STOP DRINKING
START LIVING!

Get rid of hangovers and regrets forever!

LIZ HEMINGWAY

~Freedom Publishing~

What People Are Saying About
I Need To Stop Drinking by Liz Hemingway

'I have now stopped drinking and my life has never been better! In fact it continues to improve every single day.'

'I am so much happier now. My life is back on track.'

'I am so glad that I found this book. I wish that I had found it years ago.'

Copyright © 2013 Liz Hemingway

Stop Drinking and Start Living! Get rid of hangovers
and regrets forever!

Freedom Publishing

For everyone who wants to escape the pain and misery that drinking alcohol can bring.

Your journey into a better life is worth fighting for.

This book is dedicated to you.

ABOUT THE AUTHOR

Hi there, my name is Liz Hemingway. I would like to help you escape from the misery of drinking too much and too often by sharing with you my thoughts and what I did to escape from my alcohol nightmare.

I hope to give you determination and inspiration on your journey to a better life. To know that a hopeless problem drinker like me can stop drinking and be happy can give you hope and encouragement.

This could be the last piece of the jigsaw that you need to unlock the door to your freedom. I searched long and hard for the key. I have found it and want to share it with you so that you too can wake up in the morning feeling great and knowing that you are at last free to live the life that you were born to live.

> *'You must know that in any moment a decision you make can change the course of your life forever... the very next book you read or page you turn could be the one single thing that causes the floodgates to open, and all of the things that you've been waiting for to fall into place.'*
>
> Tony Robbins

This could be that moment!

CONTENTS

INTRODUCTION

I tried to stop drinking several times before I finally managed to stop completely. I knew that I wanted to stop the horrible consequences of drinking too much and drinking too often but in the back of my mind I was not fully committed to my decision. The problem was that I could not really believe that I could have a happy, joyful, fulfilled life if I had to say no to alcohol forever. On one level I accepted this fact but on a deeper level I was convinced that I would be missing out on something.

In this book I have explored the missing link between wanting to stop drinking, feeling that you should stop drinking and actually knowing with all your heart, body and soul that enough is really enough; to reach that magical point in your life where the jigsaw pieces finally fit and it all makes total and complete sense to stop drinking. In order to arrive at this point I went through the following stages:

- ➤ I did not realize that my drinking was a problem.

- ➤ I was fed-up of the way alcohol made me feel and wanted to do 'something' about it.

> ➤ I tried to control my drinking.

> ➤ I tried to stop a few times.

> ➤ I forgot about my drinking problem for a while.

> ➤ I became aware that my drinking was still causing me hurt, shame and embarrassment. It was taking me nowhere and I could not go on like this.

The penny dropped and I finally reached that level of awareness - total acceptance and knowing. I reached that magical point where I really did not want to drink again. In that very moment I gave up my fight with alcohol. It had no power over me anymore. I cannot put into words just how wonderful that day was.

I would like you to finally reach this point and discover the magic for yourself; not just for a day or a week but forever.

I have been where many problem drinkers are right now. I have been a slave to alcohol. Every part of my life has been affected by drinking too much. I regularly woke up feeling like I just wanted to curl up and die. Mornings were often the worst part of the day for me. I have tried to express my feelings of pain, torture and failure. I went through many mornings that were similar to this one:

It is early morning. I am aware of the bright light hurting my eyes. I choose to keep them closed. It is easier this way. I can hear the birds outside welcoming the new day with their happy songs. I find the noise irritating to say the least. It is drilling into my alcohol soaked brain. I slowly curl myself into the fetal position and attempt to get back to blessed sleep. Try as I might I cannot do it. For one, I badly need to go to the toilet and also I am desperate for a drink of water. My throat and mouth are really parched and dry. I am now torn between lying in my bed and being really uncomfortable or getting out of bed and trying to make myself feel better.

I finally run downstairs and go to the toilet. I notice that I am wearing my pajamas and take this as a sign that I could not have been too bad last night. I then drink as much water as possible before running back upstairs to bed. I pull the covers over my head and try to get back to sleep.

My head is pounding and my eyes feel sore and puffy as if I have been crying. I remember drinking last night and try desperately to remember what happened. I cringe with each recollection. I decide that I have remembered enough. I turn over in bed to try to drown out these memories. I am so fed-up with myself. Here we go again. Will I never learn?

I gradually drift off to a broken sleep. I promise myself that I will never do this to myself again. I have made this promise to myself hundreds of times now.

I have often thought that one way to stop myself from picking up the bottle would be if someone invented a pill that I could take to allow me to experience the end result of my night of drinking. In other words, that would allow me to experience a full blown hangover. A pill that, for ten minutes or so, would let me experience all of the pain, discomfort and regret that I am feeling right now. I would need to take it just before I had my first drink. My drinking problem would be cured. If someone could invent such a pill then they would make a fortune! For now though I am stuck with another hangover from hell and a miserable day ahead trying to recover.

This was me several years ago. If you can relate to any of this pain then this book will help you to stop drinking and, more importantly, stay stopped so that you can experience the happiness and joy of life without alcohol for yourself.

I never thought that I would be strong enough to break free from my need to drink but I have. I have stopped drinking and I have started living. I found it hard to believe that life could be so wonderful without alcohol. I really did not think that I could break free but I have. You can too!

STOPPING DRINKING HAS CHANGED MY LIFE

If you have made the decision to stop drinking then your life will change in so many ways for the better. This book is about how to stay stopped in order for you to really reap the benefits of life without alcohol. It will help you to feel happier with your decision to finally get alcohol and all of its negative consequences out of your life and keep it out for good.

Stopping drinking is often the easiest part though. Sticking with your decision can require determined effort and be a real challenge. But help is at hand.

Your toolbox for staying sober, never having another hangover and having the best life possible, is right here. Fight back! Do not be a victim any more. Do not give in to the bully called alcohol. Learn from someone who has fought against addiction the hard way and has not only survived but has changed her life for the better.

Take this chance to change your life completely. Learn how to achieve natural highs from life! Become the person that you and your family and friends can be proud of. Reap the long term benefits of not having alcohol rule your life anymore. Get yourself back in charge of your life. Start living the life that you deserve today and best of all be happy with your decision to stop.

So you have stopped drinking and you are feeling really pleased with yourself. Your life is working better in so many ways. But that little demon is still on your back and you are finding it harder and harder to keep pushing him off! What can you do? How can you stop yourself going back into the misery of addiction? How can you keep hold of your original conviction that stopping drinking is your best option?

In this book you will find strategies that worked and are still working for me. If you have read my previous book *I Need to Stop Drinking*, then you will be aware of the horrible battle I have had with alcohol most of my adult life. It is not a pretty story and even today I find reading parts of it upsetting to say the least. If you are struggling to stop drinking then you might want to read this book first. You can get it right now at Amazon.com[1] or, if you are in the United Kingdom, at Amazon.co.uk[2].

---

[1] http://amzn.com/B00BWZEDNC
[2] http://www.amazon.co.uk/dp/B00BWZEDNC

LIVES OF QUIET DESPERATION

You are not alone. Many thousands of ordinary people all over the world are suffering at this moment in time from the pain and anguish that drinking alcohol is bringing them.

In just one online alcohol recovery forum there are over 200,000 members! They are ordinary men and women who are desperate for help to stop drinking and to stay stopped. They have reached the point where they are sick to death of what alcohol is doing to them.

In my experience, people do not tend to talk openly about their fears that they may be drinking too often and too much. They would rather make a joke about being desperate for a drink after a stressful day, knowing full well that they do not mean one glass but at least one bottle!

It is a worldwide, silent epidemic. Except for

television documentaries about young people partying, having drinking competitions and then throwing up in the gutter, the real extent of the misery that alcohol is causing is kept under wraps. People are suffering in silence, guilt and shame. They are living lives of quiet desperation. I know, because I was one of them. We all need to stand up and say enough is enough. We all deserve to live our best life possible.

My life has improved in so many ways since I stopped drinking and I never want to go back there ever. Don't get me wrong, I still have problems and challenges, we all have, but they are not nearly as overwhelming nowadays. I can cope with life so much better. I am, at last, strong enough to live a life that I am proud of. I feel in control of my life now. The most important thing is that I am no longer wasting my life drinking a poison that kept me in chains and prevented me from achieving my full potential and truly enjoying life. Every single day I am so grateful for having finally come to my senses and see alcohol in its true light.

The key to remaining alcohol free is to remember where my drinking has taken me in the past and where it will take me again if I give it a foothold. I have accepted this and problem drinkers need to understand this too. I know only too well that it is a damn hard thing to accept.

I am very much aware that many people relapse and that relapse and disaster may only be one drink away. I tried to stop drinking on several occasions before I finally got it. I would love it, if through reading this book, you finally 'got it' too and started to live a life that is not filled with regret, pain and hangovers. It is so easy to start telling ourselves:

- ➢ That one drink will not hurt
- ➢ That our drinking was not that bad in the first place
- ➢ That now we have our drinking under control we can go back to drinking socially, like 'normal drinkers'
- ➢ That we are missing out on being part of our group or that we are missing out on 'something'

When we stop drinking we can easily forget about the problems that alcohol brought us because our lives are working so much better. We want what we perceive to be more. When holidays and birthdays come around and we see all of our family and friends having fun sipping their wine or cold beer we feel that we are missing out on something. We attend a wedding and we want to toast the bride and groom with champagne, just like everyone else.

We are social creatures. We want to be part of our group. We want to be on the same wave length as our friends. We can easily forget about where alcohol has taken us and we let ourselves pretend that we can control our drinking this time.

We give alcohol a second chance to stop ruining our lives and then a third chance. Just like holding on to an abusive lover, we hold onto alcohol and come back, bruised, and battered for more.

WE FORGET THE POWER OF ALCOHOL WHEN IT GETS INTO OUR SYSTEM

Give alcohol a little foothold and it is right in there again dictating our lives. It takes us by the throat and eventually has us screaming for mercy. As I wrote in my previous book, we hold the key, but in order to use it we have to be in the correct mindset to hold onto sobriety and all of its amazing benefits.

You have to constantly work at maintaining the correct frame of mind or life will intervene and you will find yourself back where you started very quickly. It is the nature of alcohol; it takes no prisoners and is merciless. When you have stopped hurting yourself with alcohol then you never want to go back there. I can help you to stay free. I want you to have the best life without the pain of alcohol messing it up. I want you to be happy and free.

In this book I give you strategies that have worked for me and helped me keep the life that I now value so much.

> ➤ A life without all of the negative consequences that alcohol brings with it!

> ➤ A life without regret and shame!

> ➤ A life that is worth living!

> ➤ A life to be proud of!

> ➤ A life that you deserve and is your birthright!

DO I REALLY HAVE A DRINKING PROBLEM?

> *'You will not break loose until you realize that you, yourself, forge the chains that bind you.'*
>
> GARY RENARD

I have stopped drinking but do I really need to? Alcohol abuse by women has been steadily rising over the years. It is now socially acceptable for women to drink and in fact it is expected that you should have a drink at parties and other celebrations. It is the only drug that you have to make an excuse not to take! Men, on the other hand, have always been encouraged to drink in order to prove their masculinity and prowess. It is seen as a rite of passage for them.

Many people are still in denial about their drinking and some find it difficult to know for sure whether they have a drinking problem or not. Their opinion about this can change from day to day. Most people

shy away from the word alcoholic. I know that I did.
It is a word loaded with negativity and the last thing
in the world that I wanted to admit was that I had a
drinking problem, far less that I could be an
alcoholic. I still do not like to think of myself as an
alcoholic. In my opinion, it is a word fuelled with
negativity. Some people will argue that once you are
an alcoholic you are always an alcoholic. Who wants
that label for the rest of your life? Here is the
definition of Alcoholism published by the Journal of
the American Medical Association.

> 'Alcoholism is a primary, chronic disease
> with genetic, psychosocial and
> environmental factors influencing its
> development and manifestations.
>
> The disease is often progressive and fatal.
> It is characterized by continuous or
> periodic: impaired control over drinking,
> preoccupation with the drug alcohol, use of
> alcohol despite adverse consequences and
> distortions in thinking, most notably
> denial.'

The above statement is very alarming. No wonder we
fight hard not to be categorized with this group. I am
more comfortable with the term problem drinker and
feel that I can relate better with that definition. I
suspect many people who drink too much would
agree.

The slang words for someone who drinks are
derogatory too. These include wino, boozer, lush,

sponge, sot, carouser, guzzler, to name but a few. You will be able to add your own variations to the list depending on which part of the world you live in.

For someone who is drunk the descriptions are just as bad, for instance, drunk as a skunk, hammered, legless, out of her head, piss drunk, wasted and smashed. These descriptions are not very complimentary either and are just a few of the nicer words that people use to describe someone who has had too much to drink. However, I personally feel that being labeled an alcoholic is the most damning and somehow the most shaming. Even though society has become much more liberal over the years, most people, especially women, would prefer not to admit that they drink far too much and it is causing problems in their life. This might be why so many of us suffer in silence and denial.

It has been estimated that there are four problem drinkers for every alcoholic in the world today. I have found that Society tends to focus on the problems of the stereotypical alcoholic. As I have previously mentioned, problem drinkers are reluctant to be labeled and have to stand up and be counted alongside an alcoholic. Many feel ashamed and feel that they would be stigmatized if they owned up to having a problem with alcohol. Why should we feel this shame? I believe that problem drinkers were unlucky when it came to the roll of the genetic dice. We do not expect people with cancer to hang their heads in shame. We would not dream of blaming them for having the disease so why should problem drinkers blame themselves? However, we are still left with this feeling that somehow there is something wrong with us and something we would rather keep to ourselves.

This is my checklist for people who are not comfortable with the alcoholic label but feel that there is definitely something wrong. This is based on my experience of drinking too much on a regular basis, over many years. Do you really have a problem with alcohol? Are you in denial of the truth? Is it really that bad? How would you answer these questions?

Can you stop drinking after one glass or does the alcohol instantly make it difficult to stop?

As soon as I let alcohol into my body I immediately gave it the upper-hand. I had given away my power and was basically at its mercy. Once I had drank my first drink I did not want to stop. Who was I going to insult or cause to worry? How bad, both physically and mentally, was I going to feel the next day? The problems that taking that first drink ignited were totally shocking and sometimes unpredictable. The list was endless. It turned me into a person that I did not like and did not recognize. I just kept on giving it the power. Total insanity! I can see this now. I would like to help you to see it too.

Can you stop after one glass?

Can you stop after one glass but resent having to do so?

Do you drink more than you should even though you know that you will experience negative consequences the next day?

I have lost count of the number of times I went into work with a hangover from hell. Having to work all day with a hangover is horrible. My job was not one where you could take yourself off to a quiet little office and recover with a coffee. It was full on and stressful at the best of times. I just wanted the day to be over so that I could get home and crawl back into my bed or crash out in front of the television. I promised myself that I would never put myself through this pain again. I really, really meant it at the time, however the call of the alcohol was usually overwhelming and eventually I would open another bottle.

Does this sound familiar? If you drink more than you planned to, on a regular basis, without worrying about the consequences for the next day, then you have a problem.

Have you stopped drinking for a short time only to quickly return?

This is quite a definite sign that drinking has a stronger hold on you than you would like. We sometimes try to prove to ourselves and others that we are in control of our drinking and can stop whenever we like. The truth of the matter is that this is probably just an excuse to justify our continued use of alcohol to ourselves and others. In an effort to control my drinking I would attempt to stop drinking for a week or a month. I could manage the week sometimes but stopping for the month was much more difficult. When we try to control our drinking it is because we feel that it is really controlling us.

Have you tried stopping drinking for a short period of time to prove that you are in control? Did it work or did you always land back where you started?

Do not try this, just think about this scenario. If you go to a bar for 5 days in a row and drink steadily for a few hours each time, would you be able to happily leave the bar and go home for the evening?

Would you be able to stop drinking for 3, 6 or 12 months without it being an issue for you?

I think many people will probably answer that they could stop drinking but they do not want to. They do not need to go that far. They cannot envisage a life without alcohol. They believe that they can control their drinking in other ways that are not quite as radical as giving up for three months or longer. Some people will have managed to stop for varying amounts of time. If you immediately started making up reasons in your mind why this would be difficult for you to do, for whatever reason, then you may have a problem.

Have you ever felt torn between the need to give up drinking and the fact that you really do not want to stop? Are you in a real dilemma with this double thinking?

This type of thinking kept me trapped for many years. It was really awful to go through. I find it difficult to explain how bad this double thinking was. Boy, I did not want to stop drinking. What I wanted to do was to get rid of the negative consequences and keep the perceived benefits. I truly felt trapped! It was a terrible dilemma to be in. I endured years of this pain when the answer was staring me in the face. By making the decision to stop drinking alcohol I was giving nothing up! NOTHING AT ALL! I just could not see it. I did not want to believe that the only answer was stopping drinking. I was blind to the truth.

Are you torn between knowing in your heart of hearts that alcohol is taking you to a place that you would rather not be but still wanting desperately to keep it in your life?

Is your addicted side continually fighting with your sober side?

Do you try to hide the amount that you drink?

If you have ever felt the need to cover up the amount that you have been drinking then this is a definite sign of a problem. I remember pushing my empty bottles or cans down to the bottom of the bin where they would not be noticed. I would sometimes drive down to the shops in the morning to replace my husband's cans of lager or anything else that I had drank the night before. This is so that he would not give me a hard time about the amount that I had drank the night before. Sometimes I would keep the wine bottle beside me so that my friends and family were not aware of the amount of alcohol that I was actually getting through. When I was drinking I always wanted to ensure that I got more than my fair share. I just did not want my friends and family to notice.

Does any of this sound familiar to you?

Have you thought up ingenious ways to hide the amount of alcohol that you are drinking?

Do you sometimes want or have an alcoholic drink in the morning?

If you are ever tempted to have a drink in the morning or do so on a regular basis then this is a huge warning sign that you should on no account ignore. I was lucky enough not to reach the stage of waking up in the morning and needing a drink. I did not really want to start drinking until at least the afternoon but usually I held off until after about seven in the evening. If you are drinking regularly in the morning my advice would be to see your doctor for help. Come back to this book later to help you continue your journey to a better life.

Do you find yourself waiting until a certain time of day before you have your first drink?

This is just another way of trying to control alcohol and to make it behave itself. I wanted it to behave itself. It never did. The truth about alcohol is that it always gets its way. It does not matter how long you wait to have your first drink the important point here is that you wanted to have a drink in the first place.

Have you ever thought about the time that you waste, waiting until you 'allow' yourself to have a drink?

Have you ever wished the day away to get to that magic time when you can have your first drink? If you are nodding your head at this moment then this is a sign that alcohol is controlling your life.

Do you make up reasons, in your head, why you deserve a drink?

Human beings thrive on rewards. We are rewarded

from birth by our parents and carers in a variety of ways. These rewards include smiles, hugs, words of praise and encouragement and all different kinds of treats. Therefore we learn that if we are good or have worked hard then we deserve a reward. It is instilled in us from birth and when we get older we learn how to reward ourselves. This makes us feel better. We learn how to reward ourselves, instead of waiting on other people to do it. We issue ourselves with a reward if we have had an awful day at work or feel that our partner does not understand us. We reward ourselves if we have had a wonderful day. We make up a million reasons in our head why we deserve a drink. Let's face it, alcohol is an easy way to reward or console ourselves. All we have to do is open the bottle or can and pour. Then we just sit down, relax and let the cares of the world disappear. It is such an easy way to make ourselves feel better temporarily. I rewarded myself all of the time and paid the price. My reward was also my punishment. It was a high price to pay.

Are you still paying that price?

Does it take more alcohol nowadays for you to achieve your alcohol high?

Do you find that you are able to drink more now than you used to a few years ago? The more alcohol you drink, the higher your tolerance becomes and the longer you can drink without getting drunk. I used to drink one 2 liter bottle of strong cider and that would get me to my desired state of drunkenness. However, as the years progressed, this gradually increased to two bottles of strong wine and anything else that I could lay my hands on! If you are drinking more than you used to then this is a warning sign that you might need to do something about your drinking now.

Are other people commenting on how much you are drinking?

This was, for me, one of the things that eventually made me do something about my drinking. As I wrote in my book *I Need to Stop Drinking* I could pretend that drinking was not an issue. My life, on the outside, was running well enough. I had a professional, well-paid job, house and a lovely family. It was only me who had to suffer the pain of the self-inflicted hangovers etc. However, as time progressed, and my children became older, they became more aware of the state that I would get myself into when drinking. I remember early one morning when my daughter found me with my face on my laptop keyboard, fast asleep in a drunken state of unconsciousness! Cringe!! This was one of many drunken incidents that set alarm bells ringing for the people who loved and cared about me. Seeing my daughter so upset and concerned about my drinking helped to make me realize the harm, both mentally and physically, I was doing to myself. I was not only hurting myself I was now aware that I was hurting my family. Of course, it was not as easy as my daughter saying 'Mum I am really worried about you. You are drinking far too much and too often. You really need to cut down or stop altogether.' No, the road to finally realizing that I just could not drink any more was a difficult one. You see, I did not want to give up drinking, and, I did want to give up drinking! I was caught in a trap! Totally crazy, I know! I knew that I needed to stop drinking but I wanted to hang on to the perceived benefits of drinking. Why could I not see the truth?

Are your family and friends noticing how much you drink?

Do they tell you that you have had enough to drink?

Do your family hide the alcohol when they go to bed in case you drink it?

Would you want to leave a restaurant if you found out that they did not serve alcohol?

I read an article recently about Dr Wayne Dyer, the acclaimed American self-help author and motivational speaker. Years ago he used to drink beer every night. He recalls a time when he went to a restaurant with his family and discovered that, for some reason, the place he had chosen, were not serving alcohol that evening. He immediately made the decision to leave, with his family, and find another restaurant where he could have his alcohol. Later on, during the night, he had an epiphany. He had felt overwhelming shame at his actions and for putting his need for alcohol before the needs of his family. He stopped drinking.

Would you leave a restaurant and go somewhere else if they did not serve alcohol?

Do you become emotional and out of control when you have had a drink?

As my drinking progressed, and just before the light came on in my brain and stayed on for good, I began to get more emotional when I was drunk. My behavior was starting to scare me. I was using alcohol to help me deal with my unhappiness and frustration. I had issues from my past that surfaced when I had been drinking. These issues concerned events that I had not told anyone about. I had not even said a word about them to my close family. I would phone people up and want to bring up old arguments. The alcohol would give me the 'courage' to tell them a few home truths. I would write controversial things on Facebook and tag people to ensure they saw my comments. Cringe again!! I would wake up in the morning with very little recollection of what I had done the night before. I am normally calm and mild mannered, but I remember throwing a mini heater across the room after downing two bottles of wine. There was one night I remember picking up a kitchen knife and pressing it into my chest. I nearly did not include this incident as it is so embarrassing and shocking for me to think about. Why I did this I will never know. I was indeed 'out of my head.'

Are you doing things that are out of character when you have had a drink?

Does Drinking Change Your Personality?

Do you change from a mild mannered person into a monster that you do not recognize in the sober light of day?

Do you scare yourself when you wake up the next morning and realize what you have done when you have been drinking?

Do You Drink And Drive?

If you have ever had a few drinks and got behind the wheel of a car, then you have to think about the danger that you are putting everyone in. I drove a few times when I had been drinking and my blood runs cold when I think of what might have happened. Drunk driving, even once, should be enough to set alarm bells ringing!

Do You Suffer From Blackouts?

Just before I stopped drinking for good I was experiencing worse blackouts than usual. The awful part was slowly recollecting bits of my previous evening's performance or being reminded of it by my family and friends. The medical definition of an alcohol induced blackout is:

> *'Amnesia experienced by alcoholics during episodes of drinking, even when not fully intoxicated, is indicative of early but still reversible brain damage.'*

Brain damage you say? Not me! That only happens to down and outs lying in Skid Row drinking strong cheap alcohol. If I do not think about this, then it will not happen to me. Who really wants to believe that they are damaging their one and only, precious body and mind for the sake of a drink? A great time down the pub with your mates, getting legless and not remembering a thing in the morning is just a bit of harmless fun. What difference will the loss of a few brain cells make?

My daughter's friend went out for the evening with over £100 in his pocket. He eventually woke up the next afternoon with no money and no phone. He still had one shoe on but the other one was nowhere to be found. He only remembers the first half hour of his wonderful evening out! The rest of it was a total blackout. Great fun! He was lucky that he actually woke up the next morning as are everyone who drinks to the stage of alcoholic blackout. He is still drinking and still suffering the consequences including the blackouts.

Do *you* suffer from blackouts? Are they getting more frequent?

Do you feel that you are buying so much alcohol that you have to plan where and when to buy it in order to avoid the embarrassment of being talked about by checkout operators and local shopkeepers?

If you live in a large city then I do not think that this would be a problem for you. It is easier to keep the amount that you are buying hidden if you have a whole host of shops to choose from. However, if you live in a smaller town, like I do, then it will be more difficult to feel anonymous when you are buying alcohol. You wonder if the shopkeeper is thinking 'she is in here every night for wine.' It will be worse for people living in small communities. I used to get the feeling that everyone must have known how much I drank. Of course the truth of the matter is that no one really notices much, or cares; as they are too busy getting on with their own lives. But when you are constantly buying bottles of wine, or any other type of alcohol, you can feel as if the whole world is noticing.

Do You Feel That You Have To Plan Where To Buy Your Alcohol From In Order To Hide Your Addiction?

If you can accept that alcohol is causing you problems then you are ready to do something about it. But what is your best course of action? Do you really need to stop drinking or is moderation the answer?

Will I Be Able To Continue To Drink In Moderation?

'If you are trying to 'control' something such as drinking, then the problem is generally out of control.' Sarah Allen Benton

I have noticed that some books on the subject of alcohol addiction and controlling alcohol advocate moderation or controlled drinking as a viable alternative. I believe that the very basis of their theory is flawed from the start. If a problem drinker was able to modify their drinking to safe, comfortable and acceptable levels of drinking would they not have done so already? Something very real is stopping them from being able to do so. It is called alcohol. Do these people really believe that a checklist of how to moderate and control alcohol will work over the long term? Imagine the scene. You have your 'plan' for the evening so that you do not overindulge. This plan is for you to go out for the evening and have two small glasses of wine with a large glass of water in between. Perfect? Problem drinking solved! I don't think so. I can imagine you being aware of every mouthful of alcohol that you are 'allowed.' There is a good chance that you would be aware of every alcoholic drink that was consumed in your company. Generally it would be a very difficult situation for you to handle. By attempting to moderate your alcohol intake you immediately place it in the 'I really want that' category! Resentment of the 'plan' to keep you from drinking too much would quickly build up. I concede that the person attempting to moderate might have some success for a short time; however the basic problem has not been taken out of the equation. The basic problem being alcohol! One drink is too many and a thousand is never enough as a famous saying goes.

You would not tell someone who wants to get rid of the negative consequences of smoking to only have ten cigarettes a day. You know, space them out, make them last. By doing this you are keeping the addiction alive. This is the same for alcohol. Once alcohol is taken into the body then it becomes a whole different ball game. Alcohol is now in charge. When you have a drink you light the touch paper. As I have said before if alcohol is a problem for you then you should not even consider taking it into your system again. I feel really strongly about this as someone who has lived through the pain of alcohol addiction. Many people do not want to stop drinking because they want to control their drinking. In my experience it is far easier to stop than to moderate drinking.

This is what I wanted to do. I did not want to stop drinking. I wanted to stop the huge problems I was causing in my life by drinking. I was stuck between a rock and a hard place. I tried moderating or controlling my drinking on many occasions, in fact, more times than I care to remember if the truth be told. I wanted to control it, instead of it controlling me.

Here are some of the ways that I tried to moderate my drinking.

> I tried only buying one bottle of wine and getting into my pajamas at 7 o'clock in the evening. This worked occasionally but it was definitely not foolproof. Far from it! I could always ask someone to pop out to get me more wine or I could quickly throw on my clothes and go for more supplies myself. The other reason for getting into my pajamas early was to ensure that I got ready for bed and not end up waking up fully dressed in the morning.

> I thought that by not starting to drink until 9 o'clock at night would solve the problem. This worked fairly well as it meant that most places had stopped serving alcohol by the time I was drunk enough to decide that I needed more. However, often by about 9.40 pm the alcohol in my system was calling the shots and I often found myself rushing out, at the last minute, for more.

> I bought wine with a lower alcohol count. Instead of my usual 13.5% or 14% proof wine I bought a wine with a conservative alcohol count of about 10%. This tactic did not really work either. I talked myself into believing that wine which was only 10% proof did not taste as

nice and that I enjoyed the stronger stuff better. I also used the argument that the stronger wine was better value for money. I now know that the only thing it was better for was to ensure a bigger, better hangover!

➢ I tried to limit myself to drinking only at the weekends. After a hard week at work I could hardly wait for the weekends to arrive and I was wishing my life away! When Friday finally arrived I tended to start earlier. I can remember leaving work sharp on a Friday night and going straight to the supermarket. I would have a small dinner or sometimes I would say that I was not hungry and have nothing before I started drinking. This would mean that I would achieve the 'relaxing effects' of the alcohol faster. After all, I had waited all week for this pleasure and reward. I would watch television programs and need to watch them again because I had blacked out by early evening. My night often 'ended' by about 8 o'clock using this method of moderation! This control would only last for a few weeks at the most and I would find some reason for drinking mid-week again.

➢ Another thing I tried was to start drinking vodka. My thinking here was that I could add diet coke to make my drink last longer and therefore I would not drink as much. Well that was the theory anyway! What actually happened was I ended up drinking more because vodka and diet coke is such an easy way to take alcohol into your system. It is sweeter than dry, white wine and you do not realize just how much you are consuming. I further tried to control this by only buying half bottles of vodka. I even remember pouring half of a large bottle of vodka down the sink before I started my evening's drinking. This, of course, was when my resolve not to drink too much had not been compromised by the effects of alcohol. I only bought branded vodka in a bid to reduce the hangover the next day. I felt that triple distilled, top of the range vodka would be better! A more sophisticated type of hangover perhaps!!

➢ If I was going out for the evening I always had to make sure that I had a bottle of wine to come home to. If I did not have the security of this alcohol then there would be more of a tendency for me to stay out later than I had originally intended and of course drink much more. So making sure that I had something in the house to drink was another form of moderation. Another way to try to control my drinking that failed miserably.

Alcohol and moderation do not go together. As soon as you think that you need to control or moderate your drinking then this is the time that you need to stop. Initially it is a horrible proposition. Controlling your drinking seems to be within your grasp. You do not need anything as drastic as stopping altogether? Do you?

I have read books and articles stating that alcohol is

good for you and that basically you can have a glass or two a day and enjoy the health benefits. These people would not be advocating that if they had any real concept of the devastation that alcohol can have on our lives. In my opinion they are deluded. Any health benefits can be gained from taking supplements from reputable health stores.

The fact is that the only solution to the problems that drinking alcohol is bringing you is to stop.

Take away the alcohol and you will take away the problem!

It took me a long time to learn this truth. I write these words in the sincere hope that I can save you from another day of pain and misery.

After many years of making myself a human guinea pig I can now state, with some authority, that trying to control alcohol is, at best, a temporary measure, and, in truth, a complete waste of time. It is far easier to stop drinking than it is to moderate your drinking. The day that you can fully embrace that concept, without any kind of hesitation, is the day you will be free!

MAXIMISE YOUR CHANCE OF SUCCESS

You have decided that you have had enough and you need to stop drinking. You know that to try to moderate your drinking does not work and it has to be all or nothing. So you stop drinking and feel wonderful both mentally and physically. Then life steps in and your decision to never drink again is challenged in many different ways.

This is when many problem drinkers falter. It is not so much the stopping drinking that is difficult but the on-going day to day battle with stress and other things that can send you hurtling back into the arms of alcohol. You need to maximize your chances of success against the might of alcohol. You have to take massive action and have to use everything at your disposal to beat the beast.

Alcohol is a cunning, persistent opponent and you have to give yourself every chance of success. This is a fight that you have to win to regain the life that you were supposed to live.

BE YOUR OWN PARENT

This idea might be a little difficult for some people to do, but you need to treat yourself as if you were your own child. The role of a parent is to love, defend and encourage and this is what you must try to do for yourself. I mean that you must look after and care for yourself as you would your own child or loved one. I find it easy to love, nurture and treat my daughters, but find it really difficult for me to spend money on myself and buy myself things even when I desperately need them!

I would love to go back to when I was a five year old child and give myself a hug! If you have read my previous book you will understand why I feel this way. We need to learn how to nurture ourselves with things that are good for your body, mind and spirit.

If you had a difficult childhood, as I did, then you may find this particularly challenging. If you feel that you did not get the love you needed when you were growing up then the chances are that you feel, deep down in your heart, that this was your fault. You may think subconsciously that this is because you are not worthy of love. It follows on from this that if you feel that your parents did not nurture and love you properly then how can you show love to yourself?

I might be wrong, but I think that if I had been shown more love, when growing up, I would have learned to love and respect myself more. I would not have needed to turn to alcohol in quite the same way. Don't get me wrong! I love my mother and know that she did her best for me. She helped me and gave me all that she was capable of giving me. However, she was lacking in love and affection herself. With a husband as selfish as my dad, six children to clothe and feed and very little money, she did what she could with the resources that she had. As an adult, I can now understand her plight. She did the best she could and I wish that she had not died so young so that I could show her more love, than I feel I did, when I was growing up.

I have forgiven my dad. It has taken a long time to do so and, if I am honest, at times I still struggle with this. I think that he loved us in his own way but was unable to show it. He was basically a cold person. Looking back on it, I do not think that he was shown much love when he was growing up. That is sad. The saddest part for me is that he was never able to change or realize that there was something missing in his life. He was happy to work, sit in the pub, sit in his chair at home and generally watch the world go by.

I remember one of my brothers telling me that he cannot recall one word of encouragement from our father when he was growing up. I did a little better because I can remember him grunting a drunken approval at me when I had passed my exams for college. I also remember the mess he made of my certificate with his greasy fingers!

One of the ways I was able to move forward with this feeling of being unloved was by talking things out, over the years, with my brothers and sister. They suffered too and in many ways they suffered more. Telling our story to someone we can trust is a powerful way of discovering and healing our inner child.

I was the oldest and managed to escape first. I remember one of my brothers telling me that he felt that I had abandoned him when I moved out of the family home. He felt hurt and betrayed. I was shocked at this knowledge. Being young, naïve and selfish I had no real concept of the void I was leaving in his life. I was someone that he could talk to and I would support him.

Now I was living 10 miles away, on the other side of town, it might as well have been the other side of the world. Of course in the dark ages of the early seventies it was not so easy to keep in touch. We did not have the luxury of a house phone and of course the all singing, all dancing phones that we have nowadays were a long way off. I wish that I had thought about him more. Hindsight and maturity are wonderful things.

Look back over your childhood to things you enjoyed as a child. What did you really enjoy?

Many drinkers have forgotten how to enjoy themselves if drinking is not involved. I know that I had. We need to re-educate and remind ourselves that we really can totally enjoy our lives without the need to pollute our bodies and minds. We did not have alcohol polluting our systems when we were children and yet we still managed to enjoy playing and laughing with our friends. We need to find real fun and joy in life.

THE SUPPORT OF FAMILY AND FRIENDS

If you can confide in your family and/or friends then this can be very helpful. You will be able to draw strength and encouragement from them. Ultimately though the decision to stop and stay stopped must be yours. Stopping drinking to please someone else will never work. You have to be careful that you do not seek support from someone who secretly wishes that you would start drinking again to make them more comfortable about their drinking choices.

INSOMNIA

Not being able to fall asleep can be a problem when we stop drinking. This in turn can lead to stress and of course stress can lead us to finding solace in the bottle again. There are many over the counter herbal remedies that you can try. I particularly like magnesium and 5-HTP. You will have to carefully experiment and find out what works best for you if sleeping is a problem. Thankfully, when I gave my body a chance to heal, by not drinking, I did not have to use these supplements for very long.

Occasionally, I find myself wide awake at one o'clock in the morning and will use EFT to help me get to relax and get to sleep. I love EFT. The problem is that many people think that it is just a lot of nonsense and are so skeptical they will not even try it. I promise you that it is one of the best methods that you can use in your fight against addiction. It also works well for many, many other conditions and ailments. It is easy to learn, simple to use and free. As

5

well as using EFT to help me sleep I have used it to successfully combat stress, headaches and restless leg syndrome. If you are unconvinced then I urge you to open up your mind and at least give this method a try. As the saying goes you have nothing to lose and everything to gain.

Getting enough good quality sleep is an essential requisite in your battle for a better life. Sleep deprivation makes everything in life a whole lot harder. Problems can seem bigger and more insurmountable. It is not just the amount of sleep that is important but the quality of your sleep as well. I have learned that if I have too much sleep then this is not good for me. I seem to have an optimum amount of time that I need to sleep to feel at my best. I woke up this morning wide awake. I felt refreshed and ready to get up and start my day. Then I looked at my clock; 4.10 am! It was far too early to get up so I rolled over and slept for another couple of hours. When I awoke the second time I felt sleepy and had to force myself out of bed. Work out what your optimum amount of sleep is. You will find a difference when you get up if you do.

MAINTAINING THE CORRECT MINDSET AND NOT LOOKING FOR ANY OLD EXCUSE TO START DRINKING AGAIN

> 'One of life's best coping mechanisms is to know the difference between an inconvenience and a problem.
>
> Cont/d

> *If you break your neck, if you have nothing to eat, if your house is on fire, then you've got a problem. Everything else is an inconvenience. Life is inconvenient. Life is lumpy. A lump in the oatmeal, a lump in the throat and a lump in the breast are not the same kind of lump. One needs to learn the difference.'*
> ROBERT FULGHUM

Try to keep your problems in perspective. We tend to live in a world where we are surrounded by miserable people moaning about everything from the weather to the state of the economy. It is so easy to get dragged into the negativity trap. You have to guard against the 'poor me' way of thinking!

You also have to guard against the need to reward yourself after a hard week at work. Society views the end of the week drink as normal and cool. This is what everyone does. It is a socially acceptable way of not only rewarding yourself but also releasing stress. Find other ways to reward yourself that will not end up making you feel worse when you have finished.

Reasons and excuses keep us stuck on the same old path. We end up going round and round in circles and this keeps us trapped and unable to move forward. If we have a reason or an excuse for not being able to achieve something like stopping drinking then we believe that it is not our fault and therefore we give ourselves permission to fail. You find what you are looking for. If you continually tell yourself that you will never be able to leave alcohol behind because your life is too difficult then this will be your self-fulfilling prophecy. You need to change your focus. You need to make a decision that you are not going to live like this anymore.

We must step up and take responsibility for our decisions in our life. Take ownership of your life without blaming someone or something else. Seize your power back right now. Take responsibility for your life and your life will change. Create your own positive life from this day forward. Give up your limitations. Empower yourself by not dwelling on small problems and allowing them to drag you down.

MY FRIENDS ALL DRINK. I DON'T FEEL PART OF THE GROUP NOW!

A true friend will understand your decision and will support you. If you can explain to them exactly why you have reached the point where you feel that stopping drinking is your only option then they will want to back you.

I recently read about someone who had informed her friends that she would not be drinking because alcohol was making her feel anxious and was causing her to put on weight. Her so called friends pressured her into having a drink because they 'liked her drunk better.' Words fail me! Stick with people who want the best for you and will support you.

I Don't Know What To Do With My Spare Time

This is such a wonderful opportunity. When we stop drinking we suddenly have so much time on our hands. We have to work hard at keeping sober and not becoming bored. We need to take responsibility for our lives and use this precious time for fun and fulfillment. It is amazing what you will find time to do. I have started to paint. My works of art are not very good but I am improving slowly and I really enjoy it. If I stand well back from my paintings and half close one eye then they do not seem too bad!

You will definitely be able to get more things done when you stop drinking. Apart from having more energy, you will be more organized and be able to follow through on your plans. Things will not seem as overwhelming as they used to. You will be able to plan better, both in the short term and in the longer term. The sense of achievement is brilliant and this feeling of empowerment will have a cumulative effect. Success breeds success.

My Husband / Wife/ Partner/ Best Friend Still Drinks And It Is Not Fair!

This can make your decision to stop drinking much more difficult. In an ideal world it would be best if your partner supported your decision to stop drinking by stopping drinking themselves. However, if you find yourself in a situation where your partner is still drinking, it is up to you how to deal with it. Is your partner supportive of your decision? Do they have their drinking under control? You may have to make hard decisions here because you will need to protect your sobriety.

I am lucky in this respect because my husband rarely drinks nowadays. If he has two pints of beer then he is really affected by it and will begin to sing lines from his favorite rock n' roll band. A sure sign that he has had too much! Fortunately for me he hardly ever drinks and knows when to stop drinking. I know that he would stop drinking if I asked him. Because he never gets drunk, like I used to, I can honestly say that I do not mind him having a drink from time to time. However, if he was going out to the pub every night and coming home drunk I would find this really difficult to cope with.

When you are not drinking and everyone else is, you can feel left out. This can leave you feeling bad. As the evening progresses you notice that your drinking friends are getting louder and louder. The chances are they will be laughing more and the laughing is louder. Someone cracks a joke. You take a drink of your lemonade and think to yourself 'it wasn't that funny'! A half hour later you are aware that topics of conversation are being repeated. A little later someone becomes angry about a small incident that would usually go unnoticed.

All this time the group is becoming louder and more riotous and you are feeling more uncomfortable. You are sitting in the middle of this stone cold sober! You do not feel part of this group. You may feel awkward and that can push you over the edge to have a drink so that you can join them. In other words, get on the same wavelength and be part of your group again. Just think, you would be able to have a drink, relax, enjoy yourself, have fun, laugh loudly at the jokes, be escorted home, wake up slumped over the toilet and spend the rest of the day recovering from a massive hangover.

Talk to your other half or friend about how you feel. Always remind yourself of why you made the decision to stop drinking in the first place.

REMEMBERING THE HEARTACHE OF ALCOHOL ADDICTION

Reminding yourself of the heartache that alcohol has caused you is one of the very best things you can do to keep yourself on track. You do not want to beat yourself up about your past drinking exploits, but you might as well make use of them to keep you on the correct path and remember the reasons that made you stop drinking in the first place.

Remind yourself, frequently, of what you've lost due to alcohol and how alcohol makes you feel the next day. Think about the pain. Make a list of all the negative experiences that you have had due to alcohol. This really helped me. I used to read my list of painful memories when I went to bed at night or at odd times during the day. It will have the most effect if you experience the pain mentally. Don't let this turn into a loathing towards yourself, but let these memories become a loathing towards alcohol and what it has done to you. You did not choose to have this difficulty in your life. It is not your fault that you fell into the trap but now you know the truth it is up to you and you alone to liberate yourself. This is a powerful tool for you to use whenever you need to strengthen your resolve. Use it. It works.

DRINK PLENTY OF WATER TO KEEP YOURSELF HYDRATED

Try to aim for at least 2 liters a day. When you are thirsty this means that your body is already suffering from the negative effects of dehydration and you will probably be lacking in energy because of this. Drinking water helps to keep our energy levels up. When we are feeling energetic this can help us cope with everyday problems and stresses in life that could otherwise lead us back down the road of having to have a drink in order to cope. Work out the best way for you to remember to drink more water every day and watch your energy levels grow!

CUT DOWN ON YOUR CAFFEINE

'What' I hear you say! Should I lock myself away and become a monk or a nun right now? I nearly left this suggestion out because I feel that initially, when we stop drinking, it is quite cruel to suggest that we should stop drinking our favorite tea, coffee or other comforting drink. However, when you feel strong enough, it is a good idea to reduce the amount of caffeine laden drinks as they disrupt your blood sugar levels and will send you on a roller coaster of highs and lows, which can lead to your resolve weakening.

You need to keep your blood sugar level even. Caffeine creates high levels of sugar in the body. Excessive coffee drinking has a similar effect to eating foods high in refined sugar. Alcohol increases your sugar cravings, creating a vicious cycle. You need to avoid this. Be kind to yourself and reduce your caffeine slowly and only when you feel strong enough.

FIND YOUR DREAMS AGAIN AND GET TO WORK ON THEM TODAY

When I was drinking I had lots of dreams that I never seemed to be able to follow through on because drinking always got in the way. Now my life has changed for the better in so many ways. My head is clearer and I can plan better and more consistently for the future. When I was drinking I could plan to a certain extent, but these plans were always interrupted by either having a drink or recovering from the consequences of having a drink. We all have dreams and ambitions and by stopping drinking you will have taken a huge step towards making them a reality. You can use this new clarity to really get to work on your dreams and to make a difference in your world. You will amaze yourself with what you will be able to do when you stop drinking.

YOU WILL FEEL HAPPIER WHEN YOU ARE NOT TAKING A DEPRESSANT INTO YOUR BODY

I feel happier and more positive. My outlook on life and situations has improved. Alcohol is a depressant

13

STOP DRINKING START LIVING!

and it certainly depressed me and held me back throughout my life. When I look at old videos of me having a drink at a party or celebration I am generally looking miserable or in my own little world. Now that I have removed alcohol from my life I have given myself an enormous boost in the happiness stakes. Now I can remember having a good time and feel genuinely happier. I love my life.

HELPING OTHER PEOPLE TO STOP DRINKING

I have found it therapeutic to be able to lend a supportive ear to people who are suffering because they have found themselves drinking too much. It is a brilliant feeling when you have helped someone to escape from the trap. You have to be careful though, only to help people who want to be helped. If someone you know is drinking too much and you feel that you could support them, then you need to wait for them to confide in you. This is a very difficult thing to do, especially when you are witnessing a relative or a friend hurting themselves with alcohol. You can, of course, talk to them and offer your support, but at the end of the day if they do not see the need to stop, or want to stop, then helping them will be difficult.

Sometimes leading by example is the only way forward. What I mean by this is being a good role model and as Gandhi says: *'be the change that the world needs to see.'* If the problem drinker can see the positive changes in your life then this might be enough to encourage them to stop.

CULTIVATE POSITIVE RELATIONSHIPS WITH PEOPLE WHO ALSO MAKE SOBRIETY THEIR PRIORITY

I would suggest joining different forums to get help and support from people who are totally aware of what you are going through. Strong friendships can be formed and the support can be just what you need when you are feeling overwhelmed by your decision to quit for good. Cultivate friendships with people who do not drink or can take it or leave it. When I stopped drinking I was amazed at the amount of people who do not drink. If you feel that you are surrounded by drinkers you need to find sober friends.

PLAN FOR HOLIDAYS AND CELEBRATIONS

Approach holidays and times of celebration as a challenge. Enjoy breaking the associations that you have built up over the years. If Christmas is coming up and you would normally have a celebratory drink then this could lead to problems of feeling that you are missing out on something. So challenge yourself, one celebration at a time, to not only cope during this time but to have genuine fun as well.

I remember when I was going through my first year of not drinking and Christmas was coming up. I was not looking forward to it. I was going to be miserable if I did not change my mind set. In my house we traditionally play 'the once a year' family games; it is great fun but, of course, I would be normally well lubricated with alcohol by the time that we got round

15

to them. Not this time though! I was stone cold sober and I loved every sober minute. I can honestly say that I had more fun and laughter than usual. I can still remember the tears of laughter running down my face that night. To be able to have genuine fun not marred by fuzzy thinking is amazing. To top that off, I can remember taking my make-up off, brushing my teeth, going to bed, reading a book and waking up without a lousy hangover and feeling wonderful! I was able to fully enjoy Boxing Day as well. Total bliss!

I also recall another challenge, during my first year of sobriety, when I went on a cruise to celebrate a wedding anniversary. The cruise had been booked up a year in advance, before I stopped drinking for good, and included an all-inclusive drinks package! It was the best holiday of my life. I enjoyed every minute of it. No alcohol equaled no hangover which meant that every day could be enjoyed to the fullest.

Just challenge yourself to conquer one celebration or holiday at a time and enjoy the satisfaction of knowing that you are beating this demon that has dominated your life for so long!

THE D WORD

Everything in life worth achieving requires a certain level of discipline. A few simple disciplines practiced every day will reap rewards. The opposite is also true because a few errors in discipline, repeated every day, has the potential to make our lives a misery. Giving up when the going gets tough is going to land you right back where we started. The good news is that we can train ourselves to become more disciplined and form new empowering habits one day at a time. All habits are learned, and because of this, bad habits can be unlearned. We can build up these new habits by disciplining ourselves daily.

KNOWING THAT OTHER PEOPLE HAVE MANAGED TO ESCAPE

I was inspired by many wonderful people on my journey to freedom. I found many ordinary men and women whose lives and happiness had been affected by drinking, to differing degrees, who willingly shared their wisdom on a variety of forums and websites. Their insight helped me enormously. They did not judge because they knew exactly where I was coming from. Knowing that they had managed to break free from alcohol gave me encouragement, inspiration and hope.

COLLECT YOUR DAYS OF SOBRIETY AS A SYMBOL OF ACHIEVEMENT

Enjoy and relish your new freedom. Rejoice in it and hold it dear to you. Challenge yourself to go through a whole year without drinking. Get an app on your phone to count your sober days. Take pleasure in watching the counter go up and up. When I first stopped drinking I remember making myself stay awake until midnight so that I could see my counter add on another sober day to my grand total. Use every little thing to inspire you to stay on track.

DO YOU NEED TO ATTEND MEETINGS?

This is purely a personal choice. I chose not to attend any meetings. I think the embarrassment of possibly meeting someone I might have known put me off. I have always been quite a private person but this is not to say that attending meetings will not be beneficial for you. It is a matter of personal choice. I chose to use the Life Ring[3] website where I received and still receive tremendous help and support from the group.

I am now strong enough to offer support and encouragement within this forum. It is wonderful to be able to give something back and know that you are helping others to escape from their alcohol nightmare. This is all anonymous, which suits me. However, I have now made friends with people all over the world, who have conquered or are conquering their drinking problems. They are amazing people! I love the fact that problem drinkers can totally relate to each other. They can understand how you feel in a way that a normal, social drinker or a non-drinker never really can. They know the battle that you are fighting therefore they can give you some useful advice or just be supportive. The best part is that they do not judge you. I was able to draw strength and support, particularly in the early days of stopping.

Recently I became aware of another amazing support forum called Soberistas[4]. It is packed full of brilliant advice and support. Nobody will judge you there so why not check it out. Another excellent forum is

---

[3] http://www.lifering.org/
[4] http://www.soberistas.com/

Women for Sobriety[5]. Check them out online.

VISUALISE SUCCESS

Visualize what your life will be like if you manage to stop drinking for a week, or a month, or six months or a year? Really imagine and see in your mind's eye what kind of life you will be living. How much better would your life become? Not just your life but the lives of the people who love you will improve. Think about that! Really feel the emotion and the pleasure of finally conquering the demon.

When you are feeling strong and positive choose a lucky charm or talisman to symbolize your feelings of pleasure at your escape from alcohol. Hold the charm in your hands as you recall how wonderful you feel right now. Infuse it with positivity. Carry it about with you so that you can recall those feelings of strength at any time. Use it as a symbol of your power.

KEEPING A DIARY OR JOURNAL

'Writing, expressing can heal us. It can focus, support, and enhance our lives and well-being. Whether we laugh or we cry, whether through sorrow or joy, we can understand more about ourselves, and each other, through keeping a journal, diary, or diaries.'

DOREEN CLEMENT

[5] http://www.womenforsobriety.org/

This might not suit everyone but I can highly recommend keeping a diary or journal of your feelings and thoughts on the road to recovery. Until I started writing down my thoughts I was never very keen on the idea of keeping a journal. I had read that it was a good idea; I just could not see this for myself. I am so glad that I tried it. When doing this I could see patterns of thoughts emerging. I was able to analyze why and when I was feeling weaker or stronger.

Writing a journal or diary is a way of examining your feelings in order to move forward. When you stop drinking, problems do not disappear. When I was in my early days of recovery I had to deal with various difficult issues, including finding out that my daughter's boyfriend had been stealing money from us over a number of years! This was traumatic, to say the least. My first instinct was to call the police but I had my daughter to think about. She was naturally devastated by this. The fact that her boyfriend would have been quite happy to let her take the blame in order to save his own skin did not help matters.

By writing my feelings in my diary I was able to work through the stress and emotions of this testing situation. I am happy to say that we have worked through this now, as a family, and the situation has been resolved. We have all moved on. This issue could have led me to start drinking again, but by writing my thoughts down I was able to detach myself emotionally from the situation and deal with it in a better way.

I was also able to work through many other issues, gaining clarity and useful insight into what worked for me and what did not.

RECORDING YOUR THOUGHTS

If you are not too keen on writing then you can always keep an audio diary. My friend finds it easier and more convenient to do this. Most phones nowadays have a record facility or you can buy yourself a Dictaphone. The advantages of an audio diary are that you can record your thoughts quickly and easily and you can listen to your recordings when your resolve is weakening. The added advantage of this is you will be able to hear the emotion in your voice at the time of recording. This may have a bigger impact on you.

DESKTOP COLLECTION

You can keep a collection of helpful articles and quotes on your desktop which you have saved from the internet or from books etc. You can refer to your file whenever you need a bit of a boost and to strengthen your resolve. This is particularly useful because you will be able to choose items that are meaningful and relevant to your personal situation to add to your collection.

REINVENT YOURSELF

In order to become someone you've never been, you've got to do things you've never done before. I think that at some point in our lives we have to reinvent ourselves and totally enjoy the process. Each time we are successful, we have to continue raising the bar and aim for bigger and better achievements. We must find a place inside of ourselves where nothing is impossible. Use this fresh start to lose weight if you need to. Get a makeover. Throw out all of your old clothes and start a brand new wardrobe using the money that you will be saving by not drinking. Change your job. If you don't like something in your life, change it!

FIND NEW HOBBIES AND INTERESTS

Go for a cycle in the country and take a picnic. Learn how to meditate. Learn how to dance for fun and exercise. Train for a 3k, 5k, 10k, half marathon or full marathon.

Make a determined and sustained effort to lose weight. The pleasure that you feel when you can fit easily into your clothes is amazing.

Learn about Aromatherapy. Play a game. Learn a new game. This can really raise your spirits unless your family are too competitive of course. That can lead to problems and all-out war! The secret is to play the game with people who are laid back. Yes, they want to win and are competitive but do not take the whole thing too seriously!

Keep chickens. We used to keep chickens when my children were young. They are lovely creatures and you have the added bonus of the fresh, free range eggs.

Go swimming with your family or friends. The world is your oyster!

BELIEVE IN YOURSELF

One of the reasons that we find solace in the bottom of a bottle may be due to the fact that we suffer from low self-esteem. It is absolutely essential for you to build up your self-esteem to help you deal with your drinking problem effectively. Building your self-esteem will take time and effort. You may not even be fully aware that you suffer from it.

Some questions to think about:

? Do you like yourself?

? Do you think that you are inadequate compared to others?

? Do you tend to be shy?

? Do you feel useless sometimes?

? Do you wish that you could have more self-respect for yourself?

To improve your self-esteem you have to appreciate your own self-worth and acknowledge and take pride in your own accomplishments. On the other hand, you have to be comfortable with the fact that you are not perfect and will make mistakes.

You need to eliminate negative self-talk and stop putting yourself down. Try to learn how to evaluate a situation realistically and interpret it in a positive way. Make a concerted effort to stop yourself from worrying about what other people think of you. All you have to be is true to yourself and your own values.

DRINKING MIRROR

I have just found out about a phone app called The Drinking Mirror. This will give you a rough idea of how you will look in 20 years if you continue to drink at the rate you are drinking. Modern technology is amazing! Use it to motivate you and keep you on track.

PMT

If you suffer from PMT then drinking alcohol might make the situation worse. If you suffer from PMT you will probably find it more difficult to stop drinking or keep stopped over this time. For people who have been lucky enough to escape the trauma of bad PMT it will be difficult to understand how these changing hormones can have a devastating effect on your state of mind for a few days every month. I have watched people close to me turn into demons for a few days until returning to their normal, mild mannered self. It would be interesting to do a survey to see if women who suffer from PMT drink more during that time. I am pretty sure that they do. To me it is a lethal combination. When you have taken the decision to stop drinking please be extra vigilant if you suffer from PMT.

If you are a man and your wife or girlfriend suffers from PMT then you may be adversely affected when she is going through it. You might not be aware of this but it is a real problem and you could be suffering too. This stress might tip you over the edge and weaken your resolve. If you are aware that this is a problem then you can deal with the fallout more effectively.

REMEMBER THE MONEY THAT YOU ARE SAVING!

You should keep a track of the money that you are saving by not drinking. This can be really motivational in itself. You may want to save the money in a separate bank account so that you can watch it grow. The thing that I really like about this method is that you can just set up the standing order or direct debit and then forget about it. I still do this today and it is wonderful. It is just like getting free money and it is amazing how it quickly adds up. Just relax and watch the money build up week after week! Then all you have to do is decide what you would like to treat yourself and your family to. It really is a wonderful feeling!

OBSERVE DRINKERS TO STRENGTHEN YOUR RESOLVE

It is very interesting to observe people who drink and this can reinforce your decision to stop and stay stopped. Watching drunks throw up in the street or falling about the place enforces my belief in the futility of alcohol. I sometimes see people in my local supermarket with their shopping trolley full of this week's latest alcohol bargains. They can look quite respectable but often they are showing tell tale signs of alcohol abuse in their face. Their skin tends to be redder and often their noses are bigger. Dark shadows under their eyes are another indication that perhaps their alcohol consumption is adversely affecting them. I do not want to seem as if I am reveling in other people's misery. Nothing could be further from the truth. I love helping people to escape from the misery of alcohol but it is not hurting anyone if I use these everyday events to sustain and strengthen myself.

BEING CONSISTENT WITH YOUR VALUES IN ORDER TO FIND TRUE HAPPINESS

It took me a long time but I eventually worked it out. I was not happy drinking. I honestly believed, for many years, that it made me happy. The truth is that it made me miserable but I could not stop. I have found real happiness and joy by living a life that is consistent with my values. My true values are being thoughtful and not hurting the people I care about. I want and value self-respect and to be a good role model for my daughters. I do not want them to worry about me. Being aware of this has led me to a greater understanding of what my life is about and what really is important.

YOU HAVE THE CHOICE – THE POWER IS IN YOUR HANDS

So you have choices. You have the power as they say on Big Brother 'you decide'!

At the end of the day it is your life. You need to see alcohol in its true light. Only you! No one else can tell you what to do. I look upon it like this:

I know, in my heart of hearts that I have wasted too many days either drinking alcohol or recovering from its effects. I have reached a point when enough is enough! I have made my decision. The negative aspects of having a 'good time with alcohol' far outweigh the positive aspects. There are actually no real positive aspects. However, getting your mindset to this point is not easy but it is possible. I am living proof! Well, it is lucky that I am still alive after some of my drunken escapades over the years! This last sentence sounds jovial and light-hearted but I actually have a sick feeling in the pit of my stomach when writing it. Take your power and step into a better life today!

MAKE YOUR BODY AND MIND AS STRONG AS POSSIBLE

KEEPING FIT

Now is your chance! You have got alcohol out of your system. You are no longer poisoning yourself. You should seize the opportunity to make the very best of your life now that alcohol is not dragging you down. You will find it much easier to lose weight, if you need to. You will also have more energy to stick with an exercise plan.

This is an ideal opportunity for you to get yourself into peak condition. The fitter you become the easier it is to cope with the stresses and strains that life inevitably throws at you. So what are you waiting for? You know what exercise suits you best, so now that you have all this extra time on your hands you will be able to use it to improve your body.

Of course, you could join the gym. It will not cost you anything because you will be able to use some of the money that you will be saving by not drinking to pay for the fees. To be honest, I have tried joining a gym but in truth I do not enjoy it very much. If you are going to get fit you need to make sure that you are motivated to exercise on a regular basis and it must not be too much of a hassle to do. I love walking and take every opportunity to get out and about in the fresh air. I also enjoy playing badminton.

Recently I have taken up cycling and get pleasure and a sense of achievement from it. You just have to find something that you enjoy and do it regularly. I know of one woman, an ex -drinker, who could have drunk most men under the table, who has now started running. She has got into it so much that she is now training for her first marathon. This would have been nearly impossible for her to achieve if she was still abusing alcohol.

OPTIMUM NUTRITION

We need to use everything in our power to give ourselves the best chance in our fight against alcohol. When we are drinking we are constantly depleting our vitamin and mineral resources. This can make it more difficult to stay stopped. I recommend trying some of these vitamins and supplements to help you to keep your blood sugar steady and generally improve your feeling of well-being.

Balancing our blood sugar is needed so that we do not have highs and lows of energy.

CHROMIUM

This mineral will help to stabilize your blood sugar levels which is a very useful addition to your tool-box. We require small quantities of chromium to encourage the pancreas to produce insulin, the hormone that helps to control blood sugar levels and aids to stop the rollercoaster effect. You can buy this in tablet form and check the correct dosage for yourself on the side of the packet. If you eat wholegrain foods, along with plenty of vegetables and fresh fruits your blood sugar level will be more balanced.

VITAMIN B1 (THIAMINE)

If you have been drinking regularly over a number of years the chances are that you low in Vitamin B. Alcohol depletes Thiamine rapidly. When we have been drinking the body struggles to absorb Thiamine and we cannot store it. This is a double blow for the health of a drinker therefore you need to ensure you replenish your body.

Some of the best sources of Thiamine can be found naturally in the following foods: asparagus, tuna, green peas, ground flax seeds, spinach, mushrooms, sunflower seeds, black beans, dried peas, lentils, pinto beans, lima beans, sesame seeds, kidney beans, pineapple, oranges, grapes, carrots, green beans, tomatoes and kale.

VITAMIN B3 (NIACIN)

Even a slight deficiency of niacin can lead to poor concentration, anxiety, fatigue, restlessness, apathy, and depression. This vitamin helps to stabilize blood sugar. Niacin also helps the body to relax, calm down and to sleep better. Taking all of these advantages together we can see how helpful Niacin will be. Food sources of Niacin include yeast extract, fish, liver and bran.

VITAMIN B6 (PYRIDOXINE)

Drinkers tend to be low in Vitamin B6. It is therefore best to supplement this vitamin for optimum health. Some of the best food sources are oatmeal, potato, banana, chickpeas, chicken, pork, roast beef, trout, brown rice, sweet potato, sunflower seeds, avocado, tomato juice, lentils, tuna, peanut butter and spinach.

VITAMIN C

Vitamin C improves and accelerates the metabolism of the toxic by-products of alcohol. It has been shown to protect the liver. Food sources include oranges, dark, leafy greens and strawberries.

GLUTAMINE

Glutamine is one of the most important amino acids the brain uses for fuel. It improves mood, memory and concentration levels. Low levels of glutamine are common in people who suffer from depression and those who drink too much alcohol. Glutamine decreases physiological cravings for alcohol. Some of the best natural sources of glutamine are beef, pork, poultry, milk, yogurt, ricotta cheese, cottage cheese, raw spinach, cabbage and parsley. You can also take a Glutamine supplement. You will be giving yourself a much better chance of staying strong mentally as it is important to prevent your mood from dropping, as this is when relapse can happen.

LECITHIN

Lecithin helps mobilize fats out of the liver. Egg yolks, liver, peanuts, whole grains, milk, and soybeans are good sources of Lecithin.

ZINC

Drinking alcohol can cause zinc deficiency in the body. The double problem here is that this zinc deficiency may make it more difficult to stop drinking! The answer to this problem is to take Zinc supplements. Zinc will also help strengthen the immune system which will need all the help it can get to renew itself. Do not take Zinc on an empty stomach. Meat, shellfish, fortified cereals, nuts and seeds are first-rate sources of Zinc.

OMEGA 3

Many people are believed to be deficient in these essential fatty acids. Scientists have identified depression as one of the health issues that Omega 3 can help with. Oily seafood is an excellent source of DHA and EPA omega-3s which are essential for healthy hearts and brains. Some of the best natural sources of Omega 3 can be found in halibut, herring, mackerel, salmon, trout, oysters, sardines and tuna. Oils can be a good source of omega-3s as well. These include rapeseed oil, walnut oil, flaxseed oil and cod liver oil.

5-HTP

As a supplement, 5-HTP is made from the seeds of an African plant called Griffonia Simplicifolia. I really like this supplement.

It is used to increase serotonin levels in people suffering from depression, amongst other things, and used carefully can make a difference in your general feeling of well-being and in your ability to cope better with everyday stresses of life. It can also help you sleep better. Some people also use it to help them lose weight. A word of warning though if you are already taking anti-depressant drugs; 5-HTP might not interact well with them. Please seek medical advice before trying this suggestion.

MILK THISTLE

Milk Thistle contains potent antioxidants that help to repair and detoxify the liver. You need to check with your health practitioner before using this supplement.

A QUALITY HIGH-POTENCY MULTI-VITAMIN AND MULTI-MINERAL SUPPLEMENT

Taking a daily multi-vitamin and multi-mineral

supplement is good insurance to help cover all bases.

G.L Diet

Alcohol has a high sugar content. When we stop drinking alcohol we also stop putting sugar into our systems. As sugar is an addictive substance, in its own right, then it is only natural that we may try to replace this sugar in some way. This is why I recommend a low G.L diet to help you deal with possible problems. This way of eating will really help you balance out your blood sugar and therefore reduce the risk of you using alcohol to get your sugar fix. When I say a diet, I really mean a lifestyle plan. By sticking to this plan you will lose weight, stop cravings in their tracks and feel more energetic. I have used the G.L diet to successfully lose weight and to help reduce my sugar cravings. I have treated myself to a variety of recipe books and am amazed at just how tasty and versatile these meals can be.

Changing your way of eating to a low G.L diet will keep your blood sugar levels balanced and not give you so many highs and lows. If you eat a high calorie, sugary treat then your blood sugar levels will very quickly shoot up. You will feel better for a short while. Then as quickly as your blood sugar levels rose they will rapidly fall again. This will leave you tired and craving your next sweet rush. It is a roller coaster effect which will leave you exhausted and needing another sugar hit. Since stopping drinking I do my best to follow this diet. It is healthy and satisfying. Protein-packed foods, such as chicken, fish, eggs, seafood, oats, lentils and lean red meat help to stop sugar cravings. If you make sure that you also eat a wide selection of fruit and vegetables then this will help a great deal to keep your blood sugar even.

Here is a brilliant low G.L recipe that I love. I wish that I had discovered this dish years ago. It is so versatile and tasty. You can double or triple quantities and freeze individual portions to save you time.

DHAL (LENTIL CURRY)

11oz/312g orange lentils

1pt/570 ml water

2 small onions chopped

6 garlic cloves finely chopped

Curry powder

14oz can tomatoes

Vegetable stock/bouillon cube

Pinch of salt (I know that it is bad but a little salt makes a difference)

METHOD:

➢ Place the lentils in a sieve and rinse them really well with cold water.

➢ Put the water, vegetable stock/bouillon cube, onion and garlic into a large saucepan.

➢ Carefully bring to the boil and simmer for about 10 minutes. Stir the mixture carefully to prevent the ingredients from sticking to the bottom of the pan.

➤ Add the curry powder and tomatoes and a pinch of salt. Stir well.

➤ Cover and leave to simmer for about 20 minutes.

➤ Check the mixture often and add a little more water if necessary. I personally always add a little more water at this stage. You can always cook it for a little longer to thicken it up again.

You are aiming for a thick, porridge-like consistency.

This dish really fills you up and you can have it on a baked potato if you wish.

IF YOU WANT TO LOOK YOUNGER FOR LONGER AVOID SUGAR!

When it comes to controlling sugar urges, having small meals at regular intervals is a better option than going for hours without eating. I try to avoid sugar most of the time because I have found out that it accelerates the aging process.

Sugar causes something called Advanced Glycation End Products or AGES for short. This in turn affects the skin causing dark circles around the eyes and sagging skin to name but a few problems. It also damages your internal organs. I want to slow down this damage as much as possible!

Of course we are all human and it would be unrealistic of me to suggest that we never have anything sweetened with sugar, but if you can manage to cut back then this will help. This is another wonderful incentive for cutting out the booze for good. I hate to think how much sugar in the form of alcohol I have taken into my body, but I am thankfully doing something about it now.

DANGER SIGNS TO WATCH OUT FOR

Starting to resent having made the decision to stop drinking can be lethal. It can happen like this. One day everything is going along nicely in your life. You are enjoying the benefits of not drinking. Everything is making sense to you now. You are feeling the best that you have felt for a long time. You feel proud of yourself and how far you have come. The next day a tiny little thought comes into your head about how great it would be to have a drink. You quickly push it away. Don't be ridiculous you tell yourself. I am not going to throw away my three months of sobriety. I would lose too much.

However, the seed of doubt has been planted. It gnaws away at you quietly. You remember the 'good times' with alcohol. Then you decide to treat yourself to a day's shopping. Imagine the following scene.

You go out for a day's shopping. It is a beautiful day, the sun is shining and the city is full of people sitting outside and having a drink. You notice one particular table. They are laughing and joking. You think to yourself 'They don't seem to have a problem. Just look at the size of their wine glasses! If I have a problem with alcohol then so must they. Look at them. Why should they have all the fun?'

You are now watering the seed that you planted earlier. The seed is beginning to germinate and grow. Perhaps we should call it a weed. You think to yourself that one drink will not hurt. You convince yourself that you can start drinking again and will be able to control it better this time. If you are not careful then you will lose this game and be right back where you started.

Make no mistake because this can be all it takes to talk yourself into drinking again. I have been there. It is one of the worst feelings ever to wake up in the morning and realize that you have wasted all of that good work and effort. You wake up to the realization that you have talked yourself into having a drink and you have to live with the consequences. You will probably be feeling terrible, mentally and physically. You know that you have made a dreadful mistake. But how long will it be before you will be able to pick yourself up and start again? I cannot express in words how I felt when this happened to me before I finally 'got it.'

So what can you do to stop this from happening to you? Well you need to be aware of your thoughts. You have to replace them with positive ones; which you need to keep yourself strong, mentally and physically. You have to take on board and use the strategies in this book. You have to reach a stage where the life you have without drinking is so much more precious, and a million times better, than the life that alcohol addiction can offer you. You want to reach that space in your head that knows that alcohol does not work in your life. You have to understand fully and completely that alcohol has no benefits whatsoever for you. Absolutely none! You have to fully believe in your heart of hearts that you do not need alcohol to enjoy life. You have to finally 'get it.'

Writing this part has reminded me of how easily we can fall into this trap. I feel ill thinking about how I talked myself into having a drink time and time again. I am so grateful that I have escaped from the hell of addiction. I hope that this helps you, to be aware of how you can slowly but steadily allow your thoughts to take you back to where you do not want to be.

PEOPLE WHO ARE ADDICTED TO ALCOHOL COMING INTO YOUR LIFE

This is a difficult dilemma to find yourself in and could pose a real threat to your resolve if you are not careful, especially if you have formed a strong friendship with them or they are living with you. You need to be selfish and protect your sobriety. So all you can do is keep doing what makes you stronger, saner and healthier. You need to be the change and see if they choose to follow.

REMEMBERING ONLY THE 'GOOD TIMES' WHEN YOU WERE DRINKING

You can quite easily forget the nightmare that you have been through with alcohol and think of soothing yourself with just one drink 'to take the edge of.' You can find yourself becoming nostalgic about times when you were having a drink with your friends because you miss the 'closeness', 'bonding' and 'good times' that seemed to happen because alcohol breaks down our inhibitions. When I was drinking I could easily forget the agony that I was setting myself up for. Why was that? I think that the immediate thought of the 'pleasure' just totally outweighed the thought of the pain. I just thought that I will deal with the consequences tomorrow. I will bury any thought of the price that I will have to pay and concentrate on my present pleasure. Alcohol is a devious master. It tricks us into thinking that we are having a good time. And that we are building positive relationships. We just allow ourselves to be deluded and conned by it.

I watched a relative knock back the pints the other night at a family party. He wanted to have a 'good time.' By the end of the evening everyone was avoiding him like the plague. The chances are he will remember nothing about his 'good time.' His daughter, who struggled to get him home, will remember though! Replace any thoughts of missing the 'good times' by watching inebriated people 'enjoying' themselves.

STRESSFUL SITUATIONS OCCURRING AT WORK OR HOME

My friend has a really stressful job. She is a teacher and her class is particularly difficult at the moment. 'Challenging' is the professional way of describing her students! Her personal life is also very difficult just now. I can see her sinking fast. I have noticed that her drinking has escalated over the past few months. From having one glass of wine occasionally during the week and a bottle at the weekend, she is now drinking most evenings with two bottles of wine on a Friday and Saturday! She is now on and still drinking!

We all have problems in life. Problems are a part of life. It is how we deal with them that is important. The real trouble with having problems is not dealing with them head on. It is easier, in the short term, to resort to old coping mechanisms including taking the alcohol route for a short term solution. This is also known as burrowing your head in the sand. The problems are still there when you sober up and there is a high chance that you have just made them worse! By facing and dealing with your problems, in the cold light of day, you will feel much better.

Of course stress is a common part of everyone's life. We usually deal with most of our stressful experiences successfully, but it's the small percentage of problems that we have difficulty managing that can cause us real problems. It is sometimes only a small issue that is the final straw and we crack.

As we cannot avoid stress it makes sense to develop a variety of ways of handling it. There are many ways to do this.

You can take more time to organize your life better. You can take control of the ways you're spending your time and energy. You can control what and who is influencing you. You can stay away from people who cause you to doubt your decisions. It is also a good idea to give people who sap your energy a wide berth.

Try to develop a supportive network of caring people around you, because feeling alone or apart from others can increase stress. Make a real effort to keep in touch with friends. Just talking out your problems will make things seem better. Learn to relax. EFT is superb for this. Try to do something relaxing for at least 20 minutes each day.

TRY TALKING TO SOMEONE WHO UNDERSTANDS YOUR SITUATION

Make sure you have the phone number of a trusted friend at hand who will be able to support you. It is important that they will be happy for you to get in touch with them at any time of the day or night. Make sure that the friend is in fact 100% behind you in your mission to stop drinking.

This might sound a bit of a strange thing to say, but the problem with people is that we want everyone to be just like us and we want to be just like them. So if you make the decision to stop drinking then do not be surprised if your friends try to talk you out of it. After all, they do not want to be the only one making a fool of themselves when you are out for the evening.

When you start to question your own drinking then your friends may feel threatened. This happened to one of my daughters recently. She decided to give up alcohol to help her lose weight and train for a marathon. She could not believe the negative response she got, particularly from her best friend.

ARE YOU STRONG ENOUGH TO KEEP GOING TO YOUR USUAL DRINKING ESTABLISHMENT AND DRINK SOFT DRINKS?

You may have to give this some consideration. It might be an idea to steer clear of your usual drinking places until you have a few weeks of sobriety under your belt.

ARE YOU STRONG ENOUGH TO KEEP ALCOHOL IN YOUR HOUSE?

I would say that it is best not to make it easy for yourself to have a drink if your resolve weakens. If you are doubting your decision and you have a bottle of white chilling in the fridge then the temptation might be too much. Whereas, if you are tempted to have a drink, but have to make the effort to go out for it, then this might be enough to make you think again.

KNOWING WHAT TO SAY WHEN YOU ARE OFFERED A DRINK

This can be a problem for some people. When you have made the decision that enough is enough and someone offers you a drink, how should you respond? Some people are wary of saying that they have stopped drinking because they feel that it will put pressure on them to explain their decision. It can be awkward. Sometimes it is easier to just say that you are not in the mood or that you are driving. You could say that you have an early start in the morning and need a clear head. I have found that if I have a glass of something in my hand no one really notices that I am not drinking alcohol and they leave me alone. You need to be ready with your reasons though because some people will be insistent that you have a drink. Of course you can just let everyone know, from the start, that you no longer drink.

DO NOT BE SEDUCED BY THE ALCOHOL ADVERTS AND TELEVISION PROGRAMMES

Have you ever noticed that the actors on soaps seem to drink constantly in a pub, or at home and never show any signs of becoming addicted except for the occasional alcoholic storyline? The power of alcohol and the devastation of addiction is generally glossed over.

The adverts on television tell us, and indeed show us, that it is cool to have a glass of red or a chilled beer after a day's work. The advertisers never show you the result of drinking the whole bottle of red because that might put their customers off just a little! They also do not tell you about or show you bloodshot eyes, dry mouths, blackouts, accidents, weight gain or the drunken bully slapping his wife and kids. It is the advertisers' job to make you buy the stuff so they do not tend to mention the misery of waking up in a prison cell awaiting sentence for being caught driving under the influence.

However, to be fair, under their adverts is a small

piece of advice for you to 'Drink Responsibly.'[6] Of course this little disclaimer has been imposed by the government, who enjoy the revenue that alcohol sales bring, but do not want people to use up all of this money on medical bills etc. These adverts often link drinking to power, success and popularity. In fact the opposite is true. Alcohol abuse has led to thousands of business failures and people falling into debt every year. Many lives have been ruined by alcohol. We must not forget family and friends who suffer too. So do not be taken in by the media. They are selling you a lie.

NATURAL HIGHS

> 'It has been my observation that people are just about as happy as they make up their minds to be.'
>
> ABRAHAM LINCOLN

We all start using alcohol to make ourselves feel better about life. It is an easy way to get 'happy' and get high. As the months and years go by we have to start paying the price of these highs. Alcohol drains us and begins to take everything away from us. The price gets higher and higher as we get further and further into addiction. We need to replace this cruel master with better options that will make us happy and nurture us. We need to find ways of making ourselves happy that do not have horrible side effects

---

[6] http://www.drinkaware.co.uk/

attached.

Many people worry that they will miss out on fun when they stop drinking. The opposite is true. My whole life has been transformed. I am much happier and have a lot more fun. The difference is that I can remember the fun and laughter. There are many things that you can do to rediscover better ways to enjoy yourself.

You can have fun rediscovering the art of meaningful conversation. I have noticed that drinkers tend to become repetitive, self-centered and boring. The next time you are out for an evening just listen in and observe for a while. It is really interesting. When people stop drinking they are able to listen better. They have more chance of remembering that we were all born with two ears and one mouth for a reason. If you can really listen to someone then this will lead to improved, stronger relationships with family and friends.

Get a natural high from becoming healthier and fitter than you have ever been before.

Be grateful for your life and everything that you have. In other words count your blessings and appreciate all the good things in your life.

Massages are great for relaxing you and making you feel on top of the world. You do not have to pay a fortune for a massage though as you can exchange massages with your friend or partner.

Laughing is a great way to feel better and lift yourself out of negative thinking. Being able to laugh at yourself also helps.

Hearing your favorite song on the radio and singing along with it! Even if, like me, you can't sing, it is a first-class way to lift your spirits. Having a little dance at the same time is uplifting too.

Watching the sunrise with someone special can be a real spiritual, moving experience. We have so many wonderful things in life that we can take for granted if we are not careful.

Taking your child to the beach for the first time and delighting in their excitement or picking strawberries on a warm summer's day. The essence and joy of simple pleasures cannot be described in words.

Helping to deliver new life into the world like puppies, kittens, or even babies! I have been lucky enough to have been present at a few births and have had the pleasure of witnessing new life being born into the world. My dog has given birth to two litters of puppies and each time I was in awe of the fact that my dog knew instinctively what she needed to do to nurture her pups. We truly live in a remarkable world. Appreciating the miracle of life can give you a natural high.

Finding a great parking space in a crowded shopping centre can be amazing. Well this one is a golden oldie isn't it? When you are expecting a struggle to get parked on a busy Saturday afternoon at the end of a month and instead you find a prime parking spot immediately. The joy!

One of the best ways to make yourself happy is by making someone else happy. You now have more time so you can use some of it to really make a difference in someone's life.

Get out of your comfort zone and surprise yourself.

Play board games with the family. You do not need to spend a fortune on them as you can buy them cheaply at garage sales and thrift stores. If someone asks what to get you for a gift then why not suggest a board game?

Plan a movie night at home. All you have to do is buy the popcorn and soda then sit back and relax.

Join an amateur dramatics club.

Talk about your blessings more than your problems.

Challenge yourself. I went for surfing lessons in South Africa. It was exhilarating and scary but I did it. I only discovered later that, as it was misty that day, the sharks in the bay were more difficult to spot!

Appreciate nature.

Wake up happy.

Appreciate the little things in life.

Smile as soon as you wake up.

When we decide to have a drink we do so to make ourselves feel better. We have to discover better ways to reach the same objective. Just a simple flick of a switch in your brain is all that it will take to turn your life around. Find that switch and turn on the light. When we put our attention on positive things, we get and can give more. That little voice in your head telling you that you will have more fun drinking is a liar. It will do its very best to keep you in chains. Do

STOP DRINKING START LIVING!

not listen to it. Cut it off dead!

STORIES OF HOPE AND INSPIRATION

> *'From every wound there is a scar and every scar tells a story. A story that says "I have survived".*
>
> *Turn your wounds into wisdom.'*
>
> C Scott

One of the things that I enjoy doing is helping and encouraging people when they have made the decision to stop drinking. I have been in contact with many lovely people from all over the world who have decided that their lives are too precious to waste any longer. I have found that there are many similarities between problem drinkers who have had enough and want to turn their lives around. Reading about the journey of people who have realized that there is something wrong with their lives and about their ultimate victory over alcohol is heartwarming and inspiring. Here are some accounts of people who you might relate to. Their pain is real but their stories are motivating and filled with hope.

BETH'S STORY

I drank heavily for many years. One evening I found an old journal of mine from about 15 years ago. One of the entries ended with 'all I do these days is drink and cry. I feel that I am in a deep hole.' As I read that line I started to cry again. This time with tears of happiness mixed with just a little bit of sadness. I can see it all so clearly now.

My drinking was a way to cover up my true feelings. I had been hiding my private drinking on top of the very public drinking I was doing. I hid bottles of vodka everywhere. I even added vodka to beer sometimes so that it would seem like I was getting high from just a couple of beers. I was actually pleased at my cunning. It kept folks off my back. I was killing myself and deep down I knew it. Looking back I can see that I had such a self-loathing issue going on and I was never sober long enough to really think about it. I never allowed myself to think about anything much. I drowned out my thoughts and feelings in liquor. I wasn't living, I was existing.

My turning point came when, one night, I ended up in hospital. I have no recollection of how I got there. I was lucky to be alive. I was referred to a counselor. Strangely enough we talked very little about alcohol. During these sessions I learned that I had absolutely no idea how to live without alcohol. I had to learn how to deal with problems. It was frightening but at the same time it was a wonderful experience. The counselor taught me that it was alright to have feelings. She explained that I needed to prepare for when life becomes difficult. I did not use a 12 step program or attend any kind of meetings. I just stopped using alcohol to escape from my feelings. I faced my fears and learned how to live my life without alcohol propping me up. What I managed to do was to change my entire life for the better.

My life is fabulous now. I have fixed everything in my life that drinking had taken from me. I got married. I have an adorable little girl. I have moved into a lovely new home. I work hard. I enjoy my life. I feel a sense of peace, stillness and acceptance. I am grateful that I have reached this point in my life.

JENNIFER'S STORY

Another sober year has gone by. I can hardly believe it! This makes four years now. I am still very thankful for each and every glorious, sober day. I count my blessings every single morning. I know what the alternative is. If hell exists, then I managed to find it. Thank God I finally came to my senses and realized what I was doing was pure insanity. I didn't want to feel like this. I did not want to die. I just wanted to be happy. Sadly, the route I had chosen for finding happiness was killing me.

The last drink I had still lingers vividly in my brain four years later. That drink lasted for three days in a row. I do not remember very much about that last three days. I do remember at one point waking up in a strange bed, on the other side of town. To this day I cannot recall how I ended up there. I just drank continually for those days. The only other thing that I can remember doing is sleeping. On reflection, it was what I needed to do to finally find and reach sobriety. This three-day drinking spree literally frightened me to death and scared me sober. I experienced madness and finally got a complete look at how deranged my choices were. The worst of it was that I was choosing to put myself through this craziness. I needed help. It is true when they say that you have to hurt enough to finally stop. That is what happened to me.

My first year of sobriety was fairly difficult. Not because of the drinking aspect, but with dealing with emotions and worries in my life. After I finally went back to work, I breathed a huge sigh of relief and thanked God for the opportunities that lay before me.

Drinking was such a big part of my life for so long. I still think about drinking now but more in a way that you would think about a child molester, if you understand what I mean.

I resolutely believe that sobriety comes from the will and desire to accomplish it. You have to want it completely and be willing to commit to it unequivocally. If you aren't ready, nothing at all is going to work for you. Half measures in anything aren't going to get the best results possible. (No pun intended)

The most amazing thing about recovery is what you discover in life. I have discovered peace, security, trust and happiness that I have never known before. I used to be an angry person filled with resentment. I blamed everyone and everything. Nothing was my fault. I am amazed by my transformation. If I become angry at something I can let it go and get on with my life. I enjoy the process of letting go. I am also free from fear. My life was filled with fear and self-doubt. I no longer get caught up in the trivialities of life that used to devour me.

I notice other drinker's behavior and I see myself in them. I shudder at the thought. I recognize how I used to be and if I'm not very careful will plunge back into that old behavior. There was a time I didn't know what day of the week it was. Each day blurred into the next. The clarity of my life today is stimulating. I never realized what I was missing before. I suppose that you can't miss what you don't know. Today I can feel happiness and joy. I will always feel eternally grateful. I am healing and hope and pray that I continue to heal. Not every day is fabulous and plain sailing, but the good days far outnumber the bad days by a mile. This suits me just fine. I will continue to do what I've been doing. I don't want to lose what I've got. To come so far emotionally is indeed a blessing for someone like me who did their best to throw away everything good in their life. Whatever comes my way I will face sober and now have true strength to endure it. What does not kill you makes you stronger as they say.

DAVID'S STORY

I started drinking when I was 13, with my friends, after school. Drinking became my drug of choice. Drink had always held a fascination for me; my own home-made wine and my Aunt's special cider made from the apples she collected from her old apple tree.

I have lots of memories of sunny, carefree days when cider helped me to have fun. This led to a fondness for alcohol which turned to a liking for beer; a lot of beer leading to a serious habit that would impact my life in such a negative way. University days went past in a haze of drink and I spent vast amounts of money on keeping my supplies stocked up. Beer was now my drink of choice and I drank it by the gallon. It was not long before I became overweight, bloated and very much deluded that women would find me attractive. The beer helped me to sustain this fantasy.

There came a time that I was getting drunk most days. I never really felt well. I had no energy. I could not see the damage that I was doing to myself. I did not care about the worry I was putting my family through. I shut it out. I was going nowhere fast and I did not care.

In 2003, I resolved to put an end to my drinking habit for good. I had my last weekend of drinking with my mates. I had seven pints on the Friday night followed by fifteen pints on the Saturday night. On Sunday morning I crawled out of bed and went for walk to try to clear my head. I happened to see my reflection in a shop window. I felt a mixture of repulsion and shame. I told myself 'this ends now.' I knew, in my heart of hearts, that I meant it. I could not go on like this. Somehow the light had dawned on me.

I decided to steer clear of my drinking mates. This was the only way forward for me. Once I had made the decision to stop, I found that I began to feel better really quickly. My health improved at a steady rate. I started playing badminton and football. I got into running in a big way. I started with 5k fun runs and now regularly run half and full marathons. These interests gave me focus and made up for the social life that I had left behind. The weight just dropped off me. I became fit and have never looked back.

Different people find different ways to cope when they stop drinking. I took strength from becoming fitter and stronger. My old, destructive high was replaced by running and keeping fit generally. This is the best kind of high to aim for. When I started to see the results, I saw no reason to give up sobriety. I look at photographs of me back in my drinking days and I think how lucky I am to have changed my life. The difference is like night and day.

ROSA'S STORY

I did not start drinking until I was in my twenties. This is when the weight started to pile on. I went from being a size 10 to a size 18 in a short space of time. I felt ill, out of breath and depressed. The more depressed I felt the more I drank. I found myself trapped in this vicious circle. It was easier to keep on eating and drinking than it was to do anything about it. I soothed myself with alcohol and food.

Most evenings I drank pints of cider and lager. I usually finished off the evening by having the 'munchies.' This would mean eating anything that I could find. After a drink I was not particularly fussy. Drink took away my pride and I didn't seem to care. My self-esteem was rock bottom. I went to Weight Watchers in an attempt to lose weight but I was always unsuccessful because I just could not give up the booze. Sometimes in an effort to lose weight, but still keep drinking, I would cut my food intake down to virtually nothing. All of this time I was just getting fatter and more bloated. To make matters even worse, I learned that I was now suffering from Type 2 diabetes. I was horrified. My life was out of control at this point.

The event that somehow made the difference was when my friend, who I had been at school with, saw me for the first time in many years. She tried hard, but she could not hide her shock at seeing me in the flesh. She covered it up well but I knew what she was thinking. I just wanted the ground to open and swallow me up. It didn't, and I just stood there mortified. She did not know it but she had just pushed me out of my apathy and there was no going back. Something had to change. At first I felt sorry for myself and then I realized that there was only one thing for it. I went back to my slimming club and gradually reduced my alcohol intake. I am not going to lie and say that it was easy, but I was determined. Eventually I managed to stop drinking altogether. I decided that I could not put myself through this anymore and that I did not want to live this way any longer. I was sick of being sick. I lost over 56 pound in 18 months. My health and energy levels sky rocketed. My blood pressure dropped and I control my diabetes easily with my diet. I am a different woman both physically and mentally. I have more confidence and wish that I had stopped drinking years ago.

EMMA'S STORY

I have always liked to have a drink. It was only in recent years that my drinking gradually increased. I have always thought of myself as a social drinker, in fact drinking was never an issue. I used to be able to take it or leave it.

Things started going badly wrong for me when my 14 year old daughter was being bullied at high school. Kids can be nasty, cruel and thoughtless to each other. My daughter went through a rough time and I suffered with her. I could not seem to help her or get through to her. She changed overnight, from a lovely thoughtful girl, into a monster. She could not take it out on her tormentors so she took her frustration out on me. When she started cutting herself I started hitting the wine big time. I was so worried. My beautiful, precious daughter was scarring herself for life and did not seem to care! I felt powerless. I told myself that I would stop drinking as much when this whole nightmare was over. Eventually things did settle down. One of the bullies moved to another school and the other one was expelled. My daughter was able to move on and get on with her life. I was so relieved but I was still drinking every night and could not get out of the habit. My usual bottle of wine was no longer enough. I resented having to share a bottle of wine with my partner. I needed to have it all to myself. I knew that I was making myself ill and promised myself that I would cut down. The promises that I made myself usually lasted about a day at the most. My resolve just disappeared. I spent six years working on my drinking problem! I would stop drinking for a few days until the urge to have a drink overpowered me.

I think that my turning point came when I looked in the mirror one morning and saw someone that I did not recognize and did not like staring back at me through bloodshot eyes. I can't really say what made the difference that morning. It was like a sudden awakening. The funny thing was, that as soon as I had made the decision to stop drinking that morning, little synchronicities started happening. My friend confided in me that she was drinking too much and wanted to stop too. I never knew that she was being ruled by alcohol too. We helped each other. Another coincidence happened, the very same day, when I was in my local library and Allen Carr's *Control Alcohol* literally fell at my feet. The writing was on the wall!

The main lesson I have learned is that living without alcohol does not mean depriving yourself of something good and life enhancing. I have found this to be quite the opposite in fact. I am now choosing not to go on dulling my mind, judgment, senses and enjoyment of life with a destructive poison, masquerading as a bottle of fun. I know that I have not given up anything at all; I am simply choosing to have a better quality of life for myself and my family. My life has never been so good and because I am not hitting the bottle my relationship with my daughter has never been better.

KATHY'S STORY

I drank and smoked pot since the age of 17. My family were always on at me to stop. I pretended that I did not care. They knew that I was killing myself with this shit. The more they nagged me, the more I drank. I was a wild child and did not really care about anyone but myself. As long as I had my smoke and bottle of Jack Daniels then my world was a happy place. Drinking and smoking helped me to stay calm. It soothed me. It also got me involved in some of the worst situations of my life.

I finally got my act together when I was done for DUI. The night that I spent in a police cell gave me time to think. I was awake all night. What the f**k was I doing to myself? It was the lowest point of my life. Here I was, 31 years old, and everything was a total mess. I looked about 50. I felt about 80.

I got loads of help online and have made friends who have stopped drinking or are still trying to finally stop for good.

My biggest regret is that I did not stop drinking before my mother died. I have suffered such remorse over this. She died suddenly and that was so hard. Hopefully she knows that I have kicked the liquor and my life has done a 360 degrees turn for the better.

ROBBIE'S STORY

I started drinking when I was 16 because I lacked confidence and beer definitely helped to make me feel better about myself. I liked getting 'out of my box' and it did not take much to reach this level of intoxication. I was always the joker in the pack and this was the way I hid my insecurities. I did not suffer from hangovers much.

When I was younger I tended to drink just at weekends. I lived in a remote country area where the last bus home was at 10 o'clock. I got round this problem by phoning my Dad up at 2 o'clock in the morning and asking him to come and pick me up. I knew that he did not want to but my mother made him. She used to worry about me so I played on this.

Things calmed down when I got married. I still enjoyed a drink but a certain amount of maturity had kicked in by this time. My wife and I were both working hard and enjoying life. Then the kids came along and we could not get out much as a couple so I started going out to pubs by myself. I would often not be in until well after midnight and my wife would be worried sick about me. When I did get home she would try her best to get me to bed so that I would not wake up the kids.

I made her life a misery during this time. I was always sorry the next morning, but nothing really changed. I acted this way for years. I was convicted - not once but twice - for drinking and driving. You think that I would have learned my lesson but no, I got myself a bike and carried on as if nothing had happened!

During this time my Dad died suddenly. He was only 53. It was a real shock and so unexpected. He had the occasional drink at New Years but did not really like the stuff. He hated me drinking. His death made me think about what I was doing to myself and my family.

I remember listening to the radio when the song 'Whiskey Lullaby' by Brad Paisley was playing. I became really emotional when I heard the lines. 'He put the bottle to his head and pulled the trigger.' This was exactly what I was doing to myself. I wasn't living a life that I could be proud of. I was committing suicide, slowly. I hardly ever cry but I shed a tear or two that day. I vowed that alcohol was not going to take another day from me.

That was six and a half years ago and I have not looked back. I only wish that I had come to my senses sooner.

THE FINAL MAGICAL INGREDIENT OF SUCCESS

> *'By virtue of being alive, this power is yours. Like all things vital to your well-being—air and sunshine, to name a couple you already take for granted—the energy to create worlds is your birthright. You do it every day, at every second. The trick is to let go of the default "reality" you focus on now. Once you do, the minute you let go of the "reality" you were mistakenly taught it's impossible to avoid joy, peace and daily blessings. They will stalk you like Freddy Krueger.'*
>
> PAM GROUT

I wake up every morning knowing that the fight is finally over! I seriously never thought that I would ever stop drinking and be truly happy that I did! As well as finding a happier life without the need for alcohol, I have also found a magic secret ingredient to combine with this. It is the icing on the cake. When we are drinking to excess, the world is naturally a very destructive place because of the negative consequences we invite into our lives. However, when we finally break free from the curse of alcohol we are now in a position to think better thoughts. This in turn makes our world a more positive place to be. I have learned that it is important to remember that our thoughts are things. We influence our world with our thoughts. We have the choice to think in a positive way or in a negative way and both ways will influence our life accordingly.

You Can Only Have One Thought In Your Head At A Time So It Might As Well Be A Good Thought

Our natural state is happiness. Life is so wonderful and we are meant to be happy. We need to let go of negativity as much as we can and find our true purpose in life. Is it really our life's plan to get drunk every night? Is it our dream to wake up every morning feeling ill? We are all seeking true happiness and want to achieve our full potential. We have just been looking in the wrong place.

You have the power to grab yourself a better life right now. This very instant! You do not have to wait a minute longer. This is the only life that you have so make the most of it. It is your choice. By stopping drinking you are positioning yourself in a wonderful place of strength. You are in the driving seat. Take this chance to really change your life. No one has the power to kill your dreams but you. No one has the power to turn your dreams into reality but you. Use the decision to stop drinking as a positive force in your life and a springboard to jump off into an even better life.

In order to do this you must consciously control your thoughts. Of course, it would be impossible to do this 100% of the time but you should endeavor to have a positive outlook and think upbeat, cheerful thoughts as much as you possibly can.

YOUR THOUGHTS CREATE YOUR REALITY

Eminent scientists have proven that thoughts are things that actually create your reality. In other words, your thoughts and feelings form your life, and you can make yourself feel much better and increase your happiness by using this knowledge to multiply the benefits that stopping drinking will bring you. This important fact has taken me a long time to fully appreciate and take on board, but when I stopped drinking and consciously tried to see everything in a positive light the difference was amazing!

Treat each day as a gift. If you want to be happy and attract good things into your life, you have to put your attention onto the things in your life that make you happy, and not dwell on the things that make you sad or worried. Of course you cannot ignore problems but you do not need to dwell on them. Cultivate positive thoughts and outcomes for yourself and for others. We are all part of this great big universe and we get back what we put out to the world. The more positive we are about our life, the more positive our lives will become. The opposite is of course true. If you are feeling negative and down about stopping drinking then you will be inviting failure. This can become a download spiral so take care.

If you can see stopping drinking in a positive light then you will make your journey so much easier and your life will become more joyful every day. The message here is simple and it works. Be positive; do your best to uplift yourself and those around you.

YOU ARE A MAGNET AND YOU WANT TO DRAW GOOD THINGS TO YOURSELF AND TO THE PEOPLE THAT YOU LOVE

You can do this by thinking empowering positive thoughts every single day. This gets easier to do as the more positive thoughts begin to snowball and build momentum. The happier you feel, the happier that you become. Try to catch yourself thinking negatively and consciously turn your thoughts into the positive. This can be as simple as changing 'Oh no, it's raining again!' into 'It's raining. That's good. I won't have to water my plants today. I will have more time to spend with my friend instead.'

It can also be as simple as changing your thoughts from 'I am so fed-up because I cannot have a drink' to 'I am so happy that I no longer have to drink.' The world responds to your thoughts. If you think of things that you want, the Law of Attraction will oblige. The problem that most people have is that they constantly think of things that they do not want.

You need to extinguish these thoughts right away. Be careful what you think! Work hard at thinking good thoughts and enjoy watching your life get better!

Your current thoughts are creating your life right now so take control and create the life of your dreams

Since I have stopped drinking I cannot express how much better things have become. Apart from the huge benefits that stopping drinking has brought me, I also am so grateful for realizing the amazing power of the Law of Attraction. I have recently read a book called *E-Squared*[7] by Pam Grout. This is an amazing book about the Law of Attraction. I could not put it down. This book will inspire and motivate you on your journey to a better, happier life. It is also great fun to try out the experiments. I have no connection with the author, apart from a warm feeling towards her because she has written a book that has really touched me and has managed to penetrate my brain. When a book affects us in this way it is difficult to keep it to yourself.

Another book on the Law of Attraction that I love is *Ask and It Is Given* by Esther and Gerry Hicks. The combination of stopping drinking and getting in tune with the universe, by really embracing the Law of Attraction, has been amazing for me and it can be for you too. There are plenty of books on the Law of Attraction but it boils down to allowing the simple message to help and motivate you. Let it be the key to a better life for you and your loved ones. I tended to

---

[7] http://www.pamgrout.com/e-squared

overcomplicate the Law of Attraction when it is really very simple. If you want to attract happiness then be happy. You get in life what you look for. I choose to look for happiness. Happiness is contagious! I have learned that the happier I feel and the more grateful I feel the happier my life is. What you think about and what you end up getting always matches.

QUOTES I FIND USEFUL AND INSPIRING

Here are some inspirational quotes that I have come across over the years. I find quotes helpful and uplifting. They are full of truth and inspiration. I write them down and like to refer to them often. They have helped to keep me strong and they make me smile. Here are a few that I have chosen from my collection:

> *'You have the power to heal your life, and you need to know that. We think so often that we are helpless, but we're not. We always have the power of our mind.... Claim and consciously use your power.'*
>
> LOUISE HAY

> *'The best you can do for anyone is to thrive fully and be willing to explain to anyone who asks how it is that you are thriving, and what it is that you have discovered – and then, just relax and trust that all truly is well.'*
>
> ABRAHAM

*'Miracles only happen in the soul
of one who looks for them.'*
STEFAN ZWEIG

*'Until we know truth from our heart, it is just
a decision between right and wrong.*

*When it is from our heart, there is no
decision; we just do what is right.'*
MICHAEL CUPO

*'Gently and kindly embrace your truth, and
fear is replaced with peace.*

*Learn to be true to yourself and let your life
unfold, and no decision is difficult...no
obstacle insurmountable.'*
NICOLE J. SACHS

*'To bring something into the physical
world requires focusing on not what we see,
but on what we want to see.'*
PAM GROUT

*'When you quit drinking
you stop waiting.'*
CAROLINE KNAPP

'When the wine is in, the wit is out.'
PROVERB

'Assume the feeling of the wish fulfilled and act upon it with conviction. You will see more of it in your reality. Take massive, inspired action. Act upon it. Look for the opportunities for making it happen. Send directions to your conscious mind. Do it consistently.

Life happens. Stuff happens. Send out positive thoughts to keep you aligned. Always know how worthy you are. There is a higher place we can all reach.'

JOSEPH CLOUGH

'Be the change you wish to see in the world.'

GANDHI

'Drunkenness is nothing but voluntary madness.'

SENECA

'If you know someone who tries to drown their sorrows, you might tell them sorrows know how to swim.'

QUOTED IN P.S. I LOVE YOU, COMPILED BY H. JACKSON BROWN, JR.

'Love is a weapon and I prefer to kill with kindness and torment with tenderness.'

DR BERNIE SIEGEL

> *'If you have to drink and drive, drink tea.'*
> ANON

> *'For many, negative thinking is a habit, which over time becomes an addiction... A lot of people suffer from this disease because negative thinking is addictive to each of the Big Three – the mind, the body, and the emotions. If one doesn't get you, the others are waiting in the wings.'*
> PETER MCWILLIAMS

> *'One drink at a time is like committing suicide on the installment plan.'*
> THE WRATH OF GRAPES

> *'The chief reason for drinking is the desire to behave in a certain way, and to be able to blame it on alcohol.'*
> MIGNON MCLAUGHLIN

> *'If you need an excuse for why you don't drink alcohol, you could say that addiction runs in your family and you don't want to try it even once because you may not stop until you are dead in a puddle of your own vomit or smashed into the side of a mini-van with children's body parts scattered around your corpse.'*
> (This one does not make me smile but it does remind me of what I definitely do not want)
> DUANE ALAN HAHN

'The first thing in the human personality that dissolves in alcohol is dignity.'

ANON

'I made a commitment to completely cut out drinking and anything that might hamper me from getting my mind and body together. And the floodgates of goodness have opened upon me, spiritually and financially.'

DENZEL WASHINGTON

'This is one of the disadvantages of wine: it makes a man mistake words for thought.'

SAMUEL JOHNSON

'One reason I don't drink is that I want to know when I am having a good time.'

LADY ASTOR

'Drunkenness is temporary suicide.'

BERTRAND RUSSELL IN THE CONQUEST OF HAPPINESS

'Life is not a dress rehearsal, the curtain is up and you are on, so get out there and give it your best shot.'

ANON

'Alcohol robbed me of my laughter.'
THE WRATH OF GRAPES

'This life will only happen for you once so what do you want to do with it?'
B. LOGUE

'The problem is we all look at the world with a giant chip on our shoulder. All we need to do to change the course of our crummy lives is to get over our on-going grudge against the world, to actively see and expect a different reality. As it is now, we devote all our time and attention (our consciousness, if you will) to the things we do not want.

But it's nothing more than a bad habit. And like any bad habit, it can be changed with conscious and deliberate effort.'
PAM GROUT

'Contemporary research shows that happy people are more altruistic, more productive, more helpful, more likable, more creative, more resilient, more interested in others, friendlier, and healthier. Happy people make better friends, colleagues, and citizens.'
GRETCHEN RUBIN

FROM MY HEART TO YOU

> *'Speak with the knowledge that every utterance has the potential to serve as a balm for the weary soul.'*
>
> LILY VELEZ

I have tried to give you my best help and advice. However, in the end it comes down to you wanting with all your heart, soul and mind to stop abusing yourself with alcohol. The rewards are enormous and become better with every day. Step out into the sunshine of sobriety and never go back into the shadow of addiction. Here is a rundown of what I have gained. I have probably missed things out because there are so many advantages of stopping drinking but here goes:

- ➢ Since stopping drinking I have lost weight and have become much stronger mentally and physically.

- ➢ I treat myself with more respect.

➢ I have regained my self-respect and my feeling of self-worth.

➢ I feel an overwhelming sense of relief knowing that I have come to my senses and have done what I needed to do. My only regret is that this did not happen years ago!

➢ I am not wasting my time because of drinking and then recovering from the effects. I have learned that each day is a gift and is very valuable. You cannot buy time back. Time is the precious currency of life. I am able to make the most of every precious day instead of drinking myself to oblivion or recovering from a massive hangover.

➢ I have had the confidence to leave my job and start a brand new career.

➢ I feel so much better both mentally and physically.

➢ I eat better, most of the time, and use nutritional supplements for optimum health.

➢ I have stopped watching mindless soaps that that have run the same tired old storylines for years and will still be the same in 50 years' time, long after I am dead.

➢ I am more able to cope with the stresses and strains of life.

➢ My family do not have to worry about me anymore. They are proud of me. I love this benefit. My family are the most important thing in my life. I am so lucky. But what did I do? I put them through hell. My ace buddy, alcohol at my side, cheering me on! Well, not any more, I have my priorities in the correct order and they are staying that way.

➢ I have peace of mind.

Why don't you write down your own list and read it over, from time to time, to remind yourself of how far you have come since stopping drinking.

FINAL THOUGHTS

'I can see clearly now the pain has gone'

JOHNNY NASH

As a person who suffered the consequences of alcohol addiction throughout many years, and have now managed to stop drinking, I have arrived at the following conclusions:

> A time comes in your life when you finally get it. When this happens you want to shout from the top of the highest mountain 'enough is enough! I get it!' This is the point where you want to reach. This is your turning point that will lead you to peace, joy, happiness and success.

> You are here, alive and breathing, right now. It is not too late for you to fix things. You still have the chance to do what you might have done and become what you were born to be. At this very moment in time you have the opportunity to write yourself a fantastic future

which is free from regret. Do not wait a minute longer. Claim your new life now.

> We have to remember that we did not ask for this problem. Alcohol is responsible for stealing our authentic selves from us. We are reclaiming our birthright.

> You must do this for yourself and you alone. Live your life to impress yourself. The people who love you will be amazed and delighted as an added bonus.

> Trying to control alcohol will make you miserable. Concentrate your efforts on getting totally free.

> You have to stop putting alcohol into your body. You must stop giving alcohol your power.

> Alcohol gives you NOTHING it only takes from you. You will be giving nothing up except the pain.

> You must know that this is the best and only choice that you can make.

> It does not hurt to stop drinking. It is one of the most liberating decisions I have ever taken in my life! I am glad to say that I do not drink but, more importantly, I enjoy not drinking.

> Something has got to change deep within you. It is hard to totally explain, but it is a realization that all the benefits you believed that you are getting from drinking are just not true. You have to know and accept this with all of your

heart and soul.

➢ When you can truly see and believe that alcohol is not necessary for you to live a joyful, fun filled life then you will truly be free.

Leaving alcohol behind will be the start of an amazing new life adventure. This is the way that you have to view your decision. You should be happy and excited about experiencing the many benefits over the coming weeks, months and years ahead.

Stop drinking and start living!

I wish you well on your journey to a better life.

Liz Hemingway

If you found this book helpful it would be brilliant if you could leave a review so that this message of hope can reach other people who need help and encouragement to stop drinking. Thank you.

I NEED TO STOP DRINKING! – LIZ HEMINGWAY

Are you sick to death of what drinking is doing to you? Would you like to stop drinking? Are you fed-up of the horrible hangovers and that sickening feeling when you remember what you did the night before?

HAVE YOU TRIED TO QUIT DRINKING BUT NEVER MANAGED?

Liz Hemingway writes from the heart and with brutal honesty. She has experienced first-hand the devastation that alcohol can have on you. It takes over your mind and soul and takes everything it can from you, including your self-respect. Liz shares her harrowing story, starting with her life growing up with an alcoholic father. She relates how her own alcohol problems developed over the years and how she finally escaped from its clutches. Liz wants everyone who is being torn apart by alcohol to know that it is possible to finally escape from it and experience the joy and freedom for themselves.

Do yourself a favor, read this book and act on it. Your life will change in so many ways for the better.

> You will get back your self-respect.

> Your friends and family will be amazed.

> You will save an absolute fortune.

> Losing weight will be so much easier!

Find out how Liz managed to escape and is enjoying life so much more! You can find this freedom and happiness too.

What people who bought *I Need to Stop Drinking* are saying about it:

'*I Need to Stop Drinking,* written by Liz Hemingway, is an absolutely inspirational book that will change the way you think about your ability to take control of your life and learn to love it without alcohol. Alcohol is a substance that is so dangerous; it hurts you and those around you, it feels like an escape and it is definitely addictive. However, Hemingway does a superb job in this book of sharing her incredible story of how she overcame the need to drink and helping her readers learn how to do the same. The fact that the book is written by someone who really understands this particular addiction makes it powerful, relatable and moving.'

'One of the things that I enjoyed most about this book is it *[sic]* that it is real. By that I mean, the content is genuine and the advice is realistic. The book completely transparently shares the struggles that the author has encountered due to drinking and provides encouraging thoughts and advice regarding why life is better without alcohol.

It is touching to read that others have had the same challenges in their lives and been able to overcome them, and it is reassuring to hear someone who has experienced drinking problems share how positive life is when liquor is removed from the equation.'

'I strongly recommend reading *I Need to Stop Drinking* by Liz Hemingway. It is a phenomenally well written book that will open up your mind to the idea that life really can and will improve when you choose to forego drinking.

Hemingway selflessly chooses to share personal stories that really bring home the point that drinking is not a good life decision.

This book will open up your eyes to the amazing world that exists when you look at it through sober eyes and provides motivating thoughts to help you get there.'

'If you need to stop drinking this book will definitely give you the inspiration that will help you to become a non-drinker.

Liz Hemingway describes her struggle to stop drinking in moving detail. It is quite a shocking book but ultimately uplifting and gives the problem drinker hope for a brighter future without alcohol.

So if you need to stop drinking then I would highly recommend this book.'

'This book is the best hangover cure ever! I now wake up every morning feeling so happy and without that feeling of dread about how I am going to get through the day with feeling awful because I have drank too much the night before. I feel so much better mentally and physically. Thank you Liz.'

'If you need to quit drinking then this book will inspire you to do so!'

Help yourself to the life that you know that you should be living. Read this book today!

I Need to Stop Drinking by Liz Hemingway is available on Amazon.com and Amazon.co.uk.

This book is not intended as a substitute for the medical advice of physicians. The reader should regularly consult a physician in matters relating to his/her health and particularly with respect to any symptoms that may require diagnosis or medical attention. Any advice acted upon is entirely at the reader's own risk.

INDEX

93

W

Z

Printed in Great Britain
by Amazon